LEAVING IT ON THE ROAD

LEAVING IT ON THE ROAD

A Memoir

R.E. WAGNER

LEAVING IT ON THE ROAD
A MEMOIR

iUniverse books may be ordered through booksellers or by contacting:

iUniverse
1663 Liberty Drive
Bloomington, IN 47403
www.iuniverse.com
1-800-Authors (1-800-288-4677)

Because of the dynamic nature of the Internet, any web addresses or links contained in this book may have changed since publication and may no longer be valid. The views expressed in this work are solely those of the author and do not necessarily reflect the views of the publisher, and the publisher hereby disclaims any responsibility for them.

Any people depicted in stock imagery provided by Thinkstock are models, and such images are being used for illustrative purposes only. Certain stock imagery © Thinkstock.

ISBN: 978-1-4917-9228-5 (sc)
ISBN: 978-1-4917-9227-8 (e)

Library of Congress Control Number: 2016904509

Print information available on the last page.

iUniverse rev. date: 03/28/2016

Dedication

To my father, Ralph Wagner. Thank you for taking care of the boy I was, for believing in the young man I thought had been lost, and for shaping the man I hope to be. You taught me that you don't have to wear a cape to be a superhero.

Life shrinks or expands in proportion
to one's courage.

—Anais Nin

Contents

Preface

When I started my blog back in March 2013, I never considered turning *Leaving It on the Road* into a book. It was just supposed to be a way to share my cross-country bike ride with family and close friends. Few people knew the real reasons my father had asked me to join him on the road, and it never occurred to me that anyone else would be interested. And, as you'll soon read, I didn't think I had anything of value to say to anyone. In fact, I felt I'd done a pretty good job of messing up my life.

But as more miles of America collected behind me instead of in front of me, I began to see that I was learning the lessons of a lifetime. Those lessons came at me from all directions on and off the bike: from the desert, the mountains, my fellow riders and their stories, my father, the weather, the wind, my demons, and my fears. Initially I used them to pedal my way from the Pacific Ocean to the Atlantic Ocean. But they didn't stop once I reached the shore. After I finished, those lessons showed themselves again and again, often popping up in situations that, before the ride, had completely rattled me. In many ways, those lessons became my armor and my compass.

And somewhere along all of those highways and backcountry roads, I realized that my journey was no longer just about me. My story points to a universal truth: we all have moments of feeling lost, scared, and alone. At times we are filled with a dreadful sense that things are not going well on the road of life and the worst part is the feeling that no one could possibly understand or help. Even if there's someone to talk to—a parent, a teacher, or a friend—we don't want to admit that we simply can't hack it anymore. I know because I was that person, pretending to be happy while on the inside something was going very wrong indeed.

Pedaling 3,400 miles across the United States was not the hardest thing I've ever done. My greatest challenge was admitting to myself and—just as important—to others that I needed help and couldn't be alone any longer. This meant realizing that courage doesn't always look like we think it should. It often means being brave enough to take the first step to change what isn't working. It means making the tough choice to say, "I choose a better path for myself. I may not know how I'm going to get there, but I know I can't stay here."

I have decided to share my very private story with the world because I want to help those who are struggling or who think that their situations can't be changed no matter how hard they try. I am well aware that when you are looking up into the light of a faraway sky from the bottom of whatever mess you've put yourself in, that's the last thing you would believe.

I promise you that things can get better. In fact, your life can be more than you ever dared to dream it could be. But you need to make that choice, and you need to take that first step. Nobody can do it for you. When it scares the heck out of you, then you must ask for help. I am thankful every day that I finally had the courage to ask for help, and I am profoundly grateful that I am here to tell my story.

And that's why I wrote *Leaving It on the Road*. It's not just about my bicycle journey across the United States; it's about my life and about how I took the first steps to get it back again. I hope that by reading these pages, you will see what is possible for your own.

See you again after the last chapter.

—Eric

Acknowledgments

While many people encouraged, supported, and helped me turn my journey into these pages, I want to thank a few for going above and beyond.

Marty's Reliable Cycling for teaching my father and me proper cycling maintenance, for shipping our bikes, and for an awesome stationary bike to train on during the winter months.

The staff at Gold's Gym in Hackettstown, NJ—especially Tonie and Dora—for terrific spin classes.

Lorraine for her proofreading and her guidance.

Zack for his consistent patience and thoughtful consideration in helping me design my blog www.LeavingItontheRoad.com and for helping me set up my charity widget for the Alison Parker JMU Scholarship Fund.

Kelly for giving me the tools to start to take control of my life again.

Tara for help and guidance during troubled times.

My James Madison University friends for sticking by me during the tough times and for laughing with me during the fun times. I will always hold my fellow Dukes close to my heart.

My James Madison University professors, most notably my favorite teacher, Erica Cavanaugh.

The JMU Triathlon Club for pushing me beyond my limits and for introducing me to the world of biking.

The *JMU Breeze* and *Madison Magazine* for helping me get my story out.

My Mount Olive High School friends for four great years with so many memories I don't know where to start. I'd need quite a few pages to thank all of these amazing guys and girls, but they know who they are.

Patrick, one of my oldest friends, my roommate in college, and one of the best young men I know. I thank him for encouraging me to join the Triathlon Club in college. And I thank him for never leaving my side the morning I desperately needed a friend. An officer in the Marine Corps, he is the closest thing to a real-life Captain America I know.

Simon for taking a chance on becoming my friend during our freshman year at JMU and for coming with me to my NA meetings when I was too scared to go alone.

Brian for more years of friendship than I can count, for encouragement during my ride, and for relentless optimism every day I have known him.

The Drury family for years of treating me like another son and for endless encouragement during my ride. RIP, Mrs. Drury. We miss you.

The ABB team—Mike, Barbara, Karen, and Jim—for keeping me safe, fed, watered, and mobile during the ride.

My cross-country biking family for sharing the road with me, for pushing me forward when I didn't think I could ride another mile, and, most important, for becoming my friends. I thank David, Tom, Barry, Jan, Roger, Floris, George, Jim, Mark, Dan, Eric, Tim, Max, Phil, Philippe, Tom, Joe, Greg, Jody, Shane, Norman, Richard, and Gary.

My grandpa Smith, who is looking down on us from heaven with pride.

The entire Smith/Wagner family. I am a lucky man to have such amazing grandparents, uncles, aunts, and cousins.

Annie, my wonderful girlfriend, who has helped proofread and edit this book more times than I can count, who has patiently listened to me complain about how hard it is to write a book, and who has loved me unconditionally in every way possible.

My older brother, Matthew, for encouraging me to follow a passion wherever it might lead and no matter how hard it might become.

My mother, Lisa, for her endless support, for her creativity, for her hours and hours of edits, and for keeping me on task whenever I got distracted from my goals. From the day we hung up chapter titles all over the walls of our dining room, this book would never have been possible without her.

My father, Ralph. Everything I am today I owe to his offer to bring me along on the trip of a lifetime. "Another one in the books!"

Prologue: Summer 2012

I don't remember the exact date the panic seized me. Summer months sure do have a way of blending together. I'd recently graduated from James Madison University (JMU) and was working in the maintenance department at the assisted living community where my mother used to work. As I continued looking for a job in my chosen field of journalism, I was pulling in a steady paycheck every two weeks. Life should have been okay.

It wasn't.

During past summers, I'd worked at this same community between semesters at JMU. In those days, life was fun and carefree. I wasn't burdened with finding a full-time job, and the consequences of my actions during college hadn't yet caught up with me. I spent most afternoons painting railings, porches, and benches in the fresh air while jamming to handpicked playlists on my iPod. The residents nicknamed me the Dancing Painter as I happily made my way across the grounds.

Back then my mom still worked in that community, so we'd often grab lunch together. We would sit around a little circular table next to the large desk in her office and talk about school and my latest writing project. Writing has been my lifelong passion, and with a major in journalism and a minor in creative writing, my sights were set on becoming the next Peter Jennings or Stephen King. Nothing would stand in the way of my dream of becoming a famous writer and of making a difference in the world.

But the summer after graduation was very different from those earlier lighthearted years. My mother had a new job and spent long hours commuting to different communities within the company. I ate alone on the back patio, doing my best to avoid interacting with the rest of the maintenance staff. It wasn't that I didn't like the company; everyone there was kind and decent. Employees worked their jobs, paid their bills, and shared stories about the countries they'd left behind to seek better lives. But establishing relationships with these men and women gave my job a reality that made my pulse race.

As the summer dragged on and my applications went nowhere, my maintenance job started feeling too permanent. I worried I'd wake up twenty years later and realize I'd never left the building. Anger and humiliation formed one big emotional knot right beneath the place my heart beat. How had I gone from becoming the next great writer to washing out stains in carpets?

One afternoon, I carried a small stepladder and my usual cleaning supplies to a resident's room to wash a large windowpane. From the second floor, I had the perfect view of a pristine summer afternoon. The sun was shining and the sky was clear and blue. Shimmering waves of August heat drifted up from the black asphalt of the highway beyond the property's well-manicured lawns. Cars moved along the highway in hazy streaks of glinting metal. They were all headed somewhere. I wasn't.

One moment I was scrubbing. The next I felt the bottle of glass cleaner grow increasingly heavy in my hand. I struggled to wipe away the little patch of bubbly blue cleaner I'd sprayed across the thick glass. The same arms that had easily curled forty pounds that morning at the gym grew weaker and weaker until it became almost impossible for me to maintain my grip on the bottle. The heavy feeling worked its way across my upper body until it felt like chains wrapping around my sagging shoulders. My sneakers felt like weights.

At first I thought I was suffering from low blood sugar. Since moving back home after graduation, I'd been spending a lot of time at the gym. When I worked out with my headphones blaring, I could block out the growing sense of unease about my future. It wasn't unusual for me to suddenly become weak and irritable if I waited too long between meals.

But as swiftly as the thought entered my panicked mind, I dismissed it. I had just eaten lunch. I tried to shake off the feeling of crushing weight, but the chains continued to wrap themselves around me until I was forced to climb down or risk falling off of the ladder. The strength in my legs evaporated the moment my feet touched the floor. I sat on the first step of the ladder and let my head hang between my knees. The feeling of constriction across my chest grew stronger as my heart raced. Despite the brisk temperature in the air-conditioned room, beads of sweat formed across my brow. My head felt lighter and lighter as I lost the tentative grip I'd held on my faltering emotions.

There had been a time in my life when I didn't know the meaning of doubt or fear. I would wake up in the morning excited about the possibilities each new day would bring. But that afternoon while I washed windows, the crushing weight of poor decisions in the past, and the desperate early-morning phone call to my parents during my junior year in college, flooded my memories.

"I'm so sorry, Mom. I don't even know how it happened, but I can't go on like this anymore. I'm really, really scared because I don't recognize myself. I don't want to be alone, and I promise no more pretending. I need help."

Since that morning in March 2011, I'd done everything I could think of to get my life back on track. But I had to face the grim reality that something still wasn't right. As a result of certain choices in my past, I had lost faith and confidence in myself.

Sadness hung over me as I slowly regained my composure and returned to the stepladder. I knew I had to make a drastic change in my life, but I lacked the direction to take the most important step: the first one. I shudder to think where I would have ended up had my father not approached me a few days later with an offer that changed the course of my life. I was going to leave everything behind—the frustration, the anger, the bitterness over failing to live up to the ideals and the values I had set for myself, and the guilt I couldn't shake over betraying my family and friends. My father and I were going on the journey of a lifetime, not by plane, not by train, and not by car. We would travel across the United States by only one form of transportation.

A bicycle.

West

It is by riding a bicycle that you learn
the contours of a country best.

—Ernest Hemingway

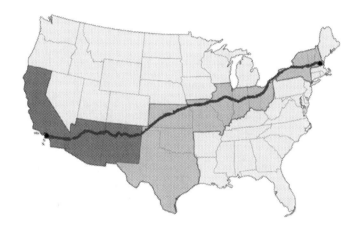

Wheels Up

BUCKLED TIGHTLY IN OUR CRAMPED SEATS, MY FATHER AND I WERE flying high above the clouds near the border of Arizona and California. Although we weren't sitting together, his presence a few rows back comforted me. Within the next half hour, our plane would touch down at Los Angeles International Airport, and once we grabbed our luggage and hailed a cab, it would be less than an hour's drive down I-105 to our motel in Costa Mesa, California. It hardly seemed possible that in less than two days we would begin our cross-country bicycle ride across fourteen states covering 3,400 miles of open road. And this would all be done in thirty-three days!

When I'd agreed to start training with my dad at the end of the previous summer, April 21 seemed like a long way off. We'd been preparing for eight months, including what had seemed like an endless winter spent riding the stationary bike in our basement or at spin classes with Tonie and Dora at the local Gold's Gym. Before starting training for the ride, the farthest I'd ever ridden a bicycle was twenty-five miles preparing for my first JMU college triathlon in Lubbock, Texas. Twenty-five miles was always the limit. Now the fantasy of embarking on such an overwhelming journey was becoming a glaring reality, and with each passing day, my heart filled with an odd mixture of excitement and apprehension.

At least we weren't the only ones attempting such an aggressive schedule. My father had signed us up with America by Bicycle, a company that specializes in supporting long-distance cycling adventures. ABB took care of all the logistics, allowing the cyclists to concentrate on the ride. There had been easier rides available through ABB, but due to my father's demanding job we'd opted for what was called the Fast America Ride.

More than twenty other cyclists had signed up to share the road with us, and with the exception of two rest days, we'd be averaging more than 110 miles each day. Aside from one man in his late twenties, I was the youngest of all the riders by far. Heck, some of them had probably been riding longer than I'd been alive. Reading about the guys who'd signed up, I learned that many had completed previous endurance rides. It was an intimidating prospect to be surrounded by so many veterans of the road.

The plane started its initial descent, and I twisted around in my seat to try to catch my father's attention. Looking completely at ease with his headphones plugged securely into the armrest, he gazed intently at his television screen. Nobody would guess that within forty-eight hours, he'd be on an odyssey few people could imagine, let alone undertake.

I stretched my arms above my head and tried to get a glimpse of the clouds past my two seatmates. I was starting to regret passing up my dad's offer to trade seats, because his was next to the window. Who knew when I might have a chance to see the West Coast from the air again? With a rueful smile, I recalled the last thing I had said to him before we found our seats. "I'll take you up on that window-seat offer on the plane ride back home, Dad," I absentmindedly called back from over my shoulder. I was too busy scanning the rows ahead for the matching letter on the ticket to my aisle seat to give my response much thought. It was only after I safely stowed my luggage in the overhead bin that I realized what I had said to my father made absolutely no sense. Our flight to California was one way. The only way I would see the East Coast again was by pedaling back.

Red Taillights

I STEPPED OUT OF THE CAB WITH MY HEAVY BACKPACK DIGGING INTO MY shoulders. Floodlights hung from the motel's Spanish tile roof and weakly illuminated its faded, whitewashed walls. While my father paid the driver, I unloaded the rest of our luggage onto the curb. The night before the flight, we emptied our packed bags and slowly repacked them, carefully checking off each item on the ABB list of suggestions. We had been given extremely specific instructions not to carry more than thirty-five pounds of luggage each, because every morning our bags would be placed in the ABB trailer and driven to our next destination. It had been a challenge, but when we finished packing, my father and I had enough clothing and travel supplies to last us for the next five weeks. I had crammed everything from toothbrushes, cycling shorts, a laptop, protein bars, bike shoes, and water bottles into the pockets of my bag. I had even tightly wrapped my bike helmet in my JMU sweatshirt and added it to the mix.

We stood quietly beside our luggage and watched the cab's red taillights slowly fade into the night. Neither of us said a word, but we were both aware of the significance of the moment. *Here we go,* I thought. Our poignant moment was quickly over when my father broke the silence with a question. "I wonder where they're keeping our bikes? Let's ask the front-desk clerk when we check in."

We hauled our bags through the sliding glass doors into the

lobby, where we were greeted by worn furniture, a well-used rug, and the briny scent of the Pacific Ocean. Despite the motel's older appearance, everything appeared neat and welcoming. A young clerk lounging behind the counter broke into a warm smile as we approached the desk. "Checking in with the rest of the bikers?" he asked, tilting his head toward the small easel next to the counter. A friendly greeting from the ABB staff was scrawled in green marker across the white board. Below the greeting was the schedule for the next few days. A meet-and-greet would take place the next morning, followed by time to reassemble our bikes, and then an orientation in the afternoon. My father was busy reading the sign, so I spoke up. "Yes. It should be under Wagner."

As the clerk checked us in, my father asked him if he knew where our bikes were being kept. We had shipped them to the motel over a week earlier, and I knew my dad wouldn't rest easy until he was sure they had arrived safe and sound. "They're probably in the Starfish Room," replied the clerk. "It's locked right now, but I'll get someone from maintenance to open it up for you." He gave us directions to the Starfish Room, and we thanked him while returning through the sliding glass doors into the chilly night. Above us thousands of stars sparkled brightly in the cloudless sky, and the only sound I heard was the rumbling of the wheels of my luggage behind me on the sidewalk.

Rounding the corner into the parking lot, I stopped dead in my tracks. Two white vans were tucked away in the lot, and even in the dim light from the street lamps, I could see the unmistakable outlines of sturdy bike racks secured to the roof of each vehicle. An ABB logo was proudly stenciled on the rear window of each van. Sitting nearby was a large blue trailer with big white ABB letters. The support vans and the trailer looked tough and dependable, and I knew they would be our lifeline to food, water, and safety for the next five weeks on the road. Once again the realization hit me as I thought, *This is really going to happen!* There was no more time for training or second-guessing. On Sunday morning my father and I would dip our back tires into the Pacific Ocean and begin pedaling east toward home.

I gave the vans and the trailer one last lingering look before heading in the direction of the Starfish Room. It was easy to spot, and I set my luggage down to wait. Minutes later, I heard the sound of rattling keys, and a man in gray coveralls came around the corner and smiled politely at us. He opened the door and clicked on the light switch. I listened as the fluorescent bulbs hummed gently to life, revealing large boxes scattered all over the room. My father waded among them, muttering, "Hmm, I don't see our bikes."

As I moved closer to two boxes hiding behind a big black case, I noticed the return address was Hackettstown, New Jersey. "Found them!" I called out. I eagerly waved my dad over, and he hurried across the room to join me. The boxes appeared undamaged with the exception of some slight fraying near the corners. "Excellent!" he said. "Now why don't we drop off our stuff and grab some dinner." He didn't have to ask me twice. My stomach was reminding me that we hadn't had anything to eat since our late breakfast.

My busy travel day started to get the best of me during dinner, and I could barely keep my eyes open. But after I had climbed into bed, sleep was hard to come by that night. In a few hours my father and I would meet the rest of the ABB riders, and the thought of so many experienced cyclists made me more than nervous.

Part of me was petrified they would all suddenly start asking me cycling questions and inevitably shun me when they discovered I didn't know all that much. What if they didn't think I could keep up and asked me to leave the ride? What would happen if I couldn't finish the hundred miles demanded of me each day? It was unbearable to consider returning home without completing what my father and I had trained so long and flown all of the way out here to do. The sense of failure would be overwhelming, especially after telling so many of my friends and relatives what we were attempting to accomplish. Several local newspapers were carrying my daily blog on their front pages, so even complete strangers would know I had failed. These thoughts raced through my restless mind as I tossed and turned beneath the thin cotton sheets.

But as the night wore on, I realized that I would rather be out on the road facing whatever challenges awaited me, with my father by my side, than lie in bed wrestling with unanswerable questions. I forced myself to focus on the reason I had come on the ride and had sacrificed almost a year of my life to train. I felt a fire in my soul that momentarily burned away the doubts and the fears. It was time for action. This was my chance to get my life back on track, and I would rather have someone scrape me off of the road than fail.

Meet the Team

Saturday, April 20, 2013—Morning

BRIGHT CALIFORNIA SUNLIGHT STREAMING THROUGH THE WINDOW told me it was morning on the West Coast. I glanced at my watch and saw that it was still early. The time zone difference must have been throwing off my internal clock, because it felt much later to me. Despite the night's tossing and turning, I felt excited as I pulled on my only pair of sweatpants and tugged my JMU sweatshirt over my head. The night's fears quickly melted away in the face of this beautiful, sun-drenched California morning. My father was already up, so we decided to eat breakfast at the motel diner since it was close and convenient.

The place was empty when we arrived except for three men sitting around a large round table near the entrance. Standing in the doorway, I watched them out of the corner of my eye, wondering if they were riders in our group. Before I could say anything, one of the men piped up. "Mornin'!" He greeted my dad and me with a warm southern drawl that reminded me of my uncle Bill, who lived in Louisiana. "Y'all here for the ride?"

"We sure are!" my father replied. After exchanging a few pleasantries, they invited us to join them. Finally, I could start putting some faces to the ABB roster we'd received a few weeks ago. I learned their names were Jan (pronounced *yawn*), Max, and Joe. Jan was the gentleman who'd first greeted us. He always smiled as if he'd just heard or told a good joke, and it wasn't long before his southern charm had us all laughing at the table like old friends. While we waited for our coffee and tea, Jan told us he was a doctor with a private practice in Alabama. He had a wife and two children, one still in college. We talked for a while, mostly about JMU, as our drinks arrived and we ordered our meals.

Max hailed from Australia and appeared to be the oldest rider at the table. His calm blue eyes missed nothing, and when he talked to you, he had a way of making you feel as if you were the only person in the room. There was a halting lilt to his accent that I found just as pleasant as Jan's drawl. Max had owned a furniture store, and after retiring, he'd taken up bike riding full time. While we waited for our breakfast, I told him about a friend of mine who was studying in Queensland, a state in Australia. Max said that he lived on the opposite side of the continent but that I should come and visit him and his wife. "We just love Americans," he said. "You're welcome anytime!" I had just met my first ABB teammates, and already I'd been invited to the other side of the world. Not a bad way to start.

Last at the table was Joe, a polite, reserved man from Massachusetts. I instantly gravitated toward his soft-spoken nature and before long we were talking about my triathlons in college and my experience on the bike. I was careful not to talk too much about the technical details. Instead, I gave Joe a rough estimate of the number of miles my dad and I rode each week to train. He told me in a quiet voice that he'd completed three Ironman races and had his eye on a fourth.

I had heard of the grueling twelve-hour race consisting of a 2.4-mile swim, a 112-mile bike ride, and a 26.2-mile run. In my mind, completing such an intense race bordered on the superhuman and the fact that Joe had done three amazed me. But when I attempted to heap praise on him, he brushed me off with a good-natured shrug. "It's just one day," he said, sipping his coffee. "Tomorrow will begin the real test, won't it?" I felt a connection with Joe that morning, but I had no idea how important that closeness would be to us both in the weeks to come.

After breakfast, Joe and Jan needed to work from their laptops for part of the day, so they left us with promises to meet up later in the afternoon. My father and I headed toward the motel lobby where we had seen the announcement on the whiteboard about reassembling bikes in the Starfish Room. Walking across the parking lot, we met another cyclist. He was tall with the wiry build of an endurance athlete. "Jody" was written on a circular nametag pinned to his chest. "Everyone is getting situated," he confirmed after introducing himself. "I just need to run back to my room for a moment."

The Starfish Room was bustling with activity when we entered. A tarp had been laid down, and several open boxes revealed bikes in various degrees of assembly. The room buzzed with the steady hum of quiet conversations mixed with the gentle clinking of metal bike parts. A freestanding rack in the middle of the room held a bike securely in its grip. Standing next to it with his lips pursed tightly and his brow furrowed in concentration, a young man with fiery red hair fiddled with the bike seat. I would soon learn that his name was Shane and that he had traveled all of the way from Ireland to see America firsthand from the seat of his bicycle.

Several other men crowded around a few folding tables covered with sheets of paper, red cycling jerseys, and several other pieces of cycling gear. I was trailing behind my dad when a woman dressed in athletic garb greeted me with a smile and a firm handshake. Her long gray hair was tied back in a ponytail, and she had the lean physique of a longtime endurance athlete. Since I knew there were no women on our roster, I assumed she was part of the ABB support staff.

"Hi, I'm Karen. It's nice to meet you," she said. "Sign-in sheets are over there by Barbara." She pointed to the only other woman in the room, who was standing behind a folding table. Several other cyclists were already gathered around it, so I decided to linger and to get to know Karen a little bit better. A retired gym teacher, she told me that she loved meeting new people and enjoyed the experiences that came with each ABB trip. After we had chatted for a few minutes, she moved on to several new arrivals.

I navigated my way over to the men standing at the table, politely excusing myself. When Barbara saw me, a smile lit up her face. "You must be one of the Wagners!" she said in a voice that felt like a warm, cozy hug, "We've heard all about you!" For a moment, I was surprised that she already knew me. But then I realized that it must be rare for a father and son to sign up for a trip like this and that people were bound to take notice.

Barbara slid a clipboard across the table, and I picked out my name near the bottom of the list right underneath my dad's name. After I had signed the form and handed it back, Barbara looked it over with a practiced eye before nodding. Swiftly, she collected packages on each of the tables and explained them to me. Apparently, riding a bicycle across the United States generated quite a lot of paperwork. There were liability forms, insurance forms, and emergency contact forms as well as instructions on helpful stretches and tips for surviving long-distance rides. Barbara handed me an official red ABB cycling jersey along with a matching do-rag that she said would help keep the sweat out of my eyes. Like a kid at Christmas, I took each item eagerly.

"One more thing," she said and handed me a blue pin just like the one Jody had been wearing. Turning it over in my palm, I saw my name written on its plastic surface. "You can pin it to the back of your bike so people know who you are on the road," Barbara explained. "Why don't you go put those things in your room and bring back your GPS for programming? Our mechanic, Jim, is calibrating everyone's routes for the first week so that nobody will get lost. And just like I told the other riders, you'll want to invest in a few handkerchiefs because we have a neat little trick that helps keep you cool during those first hot days in the desert heat."

I thanked Barbara, and laden down with my new gear, I made my way back to the room. Her words slowly sank in. The desert? There certainly weren't any deserts in or near New Jersey, and I hadn't expected to be riding in one quite so soon! But the thought of facing such a challenging environment so early in the journey couldn't dampen my spirits, especially not with all this new stuff. I hadn't been in my room two seconds before I tore my ABB jersey out of its plastic wrap, held it up, and admired it in the mirror. It was bright red, soft to the touch, and featured a drawing of America across the chest. Above the picture was the word *America* and underneath, *by Bicycle*.

When my dad walked in and saw me holding the jersey in front of my chest, he smiled and exclaimed, "Looking good! We're official now!" The words rang loudly in my ears long after I dug out the Garmin GPS from my bag. Walking back to the Starfish Room, I felt more and more like I belonged there. I was starting to feel like a real cyclist.

The first thing I noticed about Jim, our ABB bicycle mechanic, was his grease-stained apron. He reached out to firmly shake my hand, and his strong, calloused palms suggested he was no stranger to working with his hands. Yet when he reached for my GPS, he was surprisingly gentle. "The Garmin 800. She's a beauty!" He whistled appreciatively while handling the little device delicately between stained fingers. "I'm programming the routes for your first week," Jim explained.

While he spoke, his laptop screen showed map routes labeled simply Day One or Day Two. "All you have to do is access the correct date, and the route will guide you to the next stop. Between this and the route sheets you'll be getting each morning, it should be hard to get lost." (Despite his assurance, I sensed that I could prove him wrong.) Jim handed back my Garmin, and we accessed the first day. A turn-by-turn route popped up from Costa Mesa all the way to our first destination in Palm Springs. My heart skipped a beat at the end when I read the total mileage—112! It would be the longest distance I'd ever ridden in my life, and I was going to do it on the first day.

After Jim finished plugging in the correct routes for my father and me, it was time to put our bikes back together. I slipped the Garmin into my sweatpants pocket while Jim placed my father's bike in the rack. With practiced ease, he started assembling each part in its correct place. Reaching for the front tire, though, he paused.

"These wheels won't cut it on the trip," he said. "I doubt they'll even make it through the first week."

My dad and I exchanged a look; we had the exact same tires on each of our bikes. "These are very state-of-the-art tubeless tires," my father replied, his tone a bit defensive. "I bought them at a bike store in New Jersey, and they assured me they would never go flat." Jim didn't argue. But while he spoke in a serious tone, I could see a glimmer of amusement twinkling behind his eyes.

"Well, we have tires for sale if they turn out to be wrong," he said.

Shiva

Saturday, April 20, 2013—Noon

AFTER JIM FINISHED WITH MY FATHER'S BIKE, HE REACHED FOR MINE. My dad had given me the bike during my freshman year in college when I announced I was joining the JMU Triathlon Club. He told me he'd been thinking about upgrading to a lighter road bike anyway, so the timing was perfect. There were no questions or hesitations. My dad saw I'd taken an interest in something that could benefit me, and within a month I was the proud owner of his old silver Cannondale CAAD8 road bike.

I'd no idea at the time that many considered this model to be one of the best entry-level road bikes an amateur cyclist could own. It is made of a mixture of aluminum and carbon fiber. The aluminum frame is tough, yet light, built using Cannondale's double-pass, smooth-weld technology in which high-intensity lasers pass over the welding twice. This process allows the frame to be light without sacrificing strength or durability. In designing the CAAD8, Cannondale combined more than thirty years of aluminum frame technology with the geometry of its most efficient racing bike, the SuperSix Evo. My bike is so light I can almost lift it off the ground with two fingers.

I didn't decide to name my bike until I was certain that my cross-country trip was going to happen. The idea came to me while I was training on the stationary bike in my basement for what seemed like the hundredth time while watching one of my favorite movies, *Forrest Gump.* I liked to ride to *Forrest Gump* for a few reasons. I hated having to dismount or to switch movies, and it is a hefty 142 minutes long. It offers an inspirational message about a simple man achieving great things in his life. The film also provided me with a motivational game: every time Forrest ran across the screen, I increased the resistance on the bike, stood up on the pedals, and sprinted like crazy. It was a fun game, because Forrest was always running somewhere—away from bullies with braces on his legs, down a college football field, through the flaming jungles of Vietnam, or across the roads of the United States.

One day I was watching the scene in which Forrest has returned from yet another fruitless day at sea with his new shrimping boat. His efforts have yielded a measly five shrimp, but a salty old fisherman on the dock gives him an idea that changes everything. "You ever think about naming this old boat?" the fisherman asks. "It's bad luck to have a boat without a name." And with that advice, Forrest gives his boat the only name in the world that matters to him—Jenny.

I've never been a superstitious person, but something in that scene stuck with me. I knew I wouldn't be comfortable on a cross-country journey if my Cannondale didn't have a proper name. I thought long and hard before deciding on Shiva, the Hindu goddess of destruction. I could have gone with some familiar girl's name that guys give their cars or boats, but I wanted a name with more clout. Shiva is most widely known as a destroyer, but this deity is also responsible for creation. You cannot have one without the other, and to create a new life for myself I needed to destroy my old one, filled as it was with self-doubt and hang-ups. *After all,* I told myself, *wasn't that the purpose of this ride?*

I watched as Jim gently took Shiva out of the cardboard box and put her on the bike rack. Without her wheels, chain, gears, or seat, she looked like a pitiful hunk of welded metal and carbon fiber. Jim deftly fit her pieces together with confident hands, tightening bolts here and there. I quickly learned that he loved sharing stories about his time on the road with ABB, and once I saw he could chat and expertly handle Shiva's parts at the same time, I enjoyed listening to him tell interesting and often hilarious tales in his baritone voice. When Jim got to my tubeless tires, he respectfully didn't say a word, but I knew exactly what he was thinking.

Finally, he handed my bike over to me. "Make sure you wear a helmet if you go out today," he said, turning his attention to the next rider. I nodded gratefully and took hold of Shiva, marveling once again at how light she felt in my grip. It had been more than a week since I'd taken her on a ride, and now that she was whole again, all I wanted to do was get her back on the road so I could stretch my legs under the bright California sunshine. The schedule on the whiteboard said nothing else was happening until orientation at three in the afternoon. My dad must have been thinking along the same lines, because when I walked into our room with Shiva in tow, he was pulling on a pair of cycling shorts.

"Some of the other guys are going for a ride," he said. "I thought we could join them and give our bikes a test ride to make sure everything is working."

I was still uncomfortable at the prospect of sharing the road with new people, but I knew I needed to get over that obstacle in a big hurry. Besides, it was a gorgeous day and this could be my only chance to explore Costa Mesa. When we left the room, I looked down into the parking lot and saw the three other cyclists who'd ride with us. I didn't recognize any of them from the Starfish Room, but as I watched them pedal around the parking lot, I could tell they all knew how to handle themselves on a bike.

We all introduced ourselves as my father and I locked into our pedals. The first rider was George. He was a proud British cyclist who wore a powder-blue cycling uniform that was his club jersey. He owned three identical sets, complete with a little rider's cap sporting a small brim. (For the longest time I thought he was meticulous about keeping one jersey extremely clean.) George rode over to me and grabbed one of my biceps. "These arms, mate!" he joked as a way of greeting. "Good for girls but not for cycling!" It wasn't until we were climbing the steep mountains of Arizona that I appreciated exactly what he meant.

George, my dad and I, and the two other riders, Barry and Tim, hit the road and took in the scenic beauty of Costa Mesa. Everywhere I looked I saw pristine beaches and volleyball courts. I felt fresh and eager as we rode, pausing every now and then to take photographs. We stopped for a lunch of fish tacos near one of the piers and listened to a guitarist sitting on the edge of a fountain, playing classic rock songs. Growing up, I'd embraced my mother's love for music, and she joked that my brother Matthew and I could sing the lyrics to the Eagles' "Best of My Love," Journey's "Don't Stop Believing," or Carole King's "It's Too Late" before we could read. I tried to pay attention to the conversations around me, but the songs made me think of home, and I considered how far away I was from anything familiar.

Finishing lunch, my dad and I stopped at a store on the way back to buy a few bandannas as Barbara had suggested. She told us one of the best ways to beat the heat was to fill a bandanna with ice and to tie it around our necks. I bought a yellow and a purple one in honor of my JMU school colors, and my dad bought a blue one. Buying the bandannas would indeed prove to be a smart decision during the first few days as we rode through the scorching hot deserts of the outlying California countryside and eventually the sweltering deserts of Arizona and New Mexico.

By the time we returned to the parking lot, the orientation was soon to begin, so we headed to our room to change. I pulled out my neon-green "Wagner's Warriors" T-shirt with the breast-cancer pink ribbon. My aunt Donna was in the middle of a tough battle with recently diagnosed breast cancer and the whole Wagner family had T-shirts. My father and I made sure she knew we'd be wearing ours as we rode across the county. My mother always told me that when you think you have it bad, there's always someone else who has it worse. She was right.

Before heading downstairs to join the others, I looked at myself in the mirror. A naïve twenty-two-year-old looked back at me with apprehension in his eyes. It was time to meet the rest of my teammates. I flicked off the light, and my reflection was lost in the shadows.

Hello, My Name is Eric

THE STARFISH ROOM HAD BEEN COMPLETELY REARRANGED FOR OUR orientation. Gone were all the partially unpacked crates and the scattered bicycle parts, replaced by dozens of armless chairs arranged in ordered rows. At the front of the room was a large projector screen with a podium waiting for a speaker. As my dad and I found two seats near the back row, a feeling of déjà vu swept over me. I remembered this same excitement during my freshman orientation at college, but instead of a professor wearing glasses and a tweed jacket, a tough-looking gentleman stood surveying the group.

I'd briefly met Mike Munk, our ABB leader, earlier in the day while Jim was reassembling Shiva. I'd watched and listened as he politely but firmly told an upset rider he was not allowed to use headphones or listen to music at any time while riding his bike. Safety was his first priority, Mike had said, and no rider was going to even slightly jeopardize his own or anyone else's safety on the road—not on this ride, not on his watch.

Mike had a wiry build and a personality that radiated inner strength and discipline. I could tell the moment he looked at me with the same focused gaze my father had that he was ex-military. My father had been an airborne ranger in the US Army while Mike had been an officer in the US Air Force. They both carried themselves with a calm, self-assured demeanor that could turn hard as steel in an instant if the situation demanded it. With my father at my side and Mike as our ride leader, I felt very safe.

Soon the room was filled with riders, and as the orientation and introductions drew near, I swallowed hard against my growing nervousness. I used to love being in front of a crowd. In high school I was voted Most Theatrical in my senior class and had performed confidently in plays and musicals since eighth grade. I had been Daddy Warbucks in *Annie*, had emceed the Mount Olive High School Marauder Day to benefit the fight against Huntington's disease, and had sung and danced my way through two Mr. Mount Olive contests. But that was the Eric Wagner I vaguely remembered, and I hadn't seen him in such a long time I wasn't sure if he still existed.

The small talk among the riders ended as Mike introduced the rest of the ABB staff—his wife, Barbara; Karen; and Jim. Photos of cyclists riding and videos of proper technique while on the road appeared on the projector screen as he spoke about safety. One video on properly navigating highways caught my attention. I assumed we would be riding on America's backcountry roads, not sharing major highways with eighteen-wheelers and tractor-trailers. Obviously I assumed wrong.

My palms began to sweat when Mike finished his presentation and asked each of us to stand up, to talk a little bit about ourselves, and to briefly explain why we'd signed up for this trip. I learned that some of the men had traveled from as far away as the Netherlands and Israel to experience this bike ride. Several were riding to raise money for charities, but the rider who made me sit up straighter and listen more closely was Barry. We'd ridden together around Costa Mesa earlier in the day, but he'd been so quiet I still didn't know much about him. But as he courageously shared his story, I learned that Barry had been diagnosed with hemophilia at a young age. At the time, even the most advanced treatments for the condition sometimes did more harm than good, and during a routine blood transfusion, Barry contracted HIV.

After many difficult years and a long series of health complications related to both conditions, his doctors suggested that he get his affairs in order. Barry refused to give up, and as luck, fate, or faith would have it, he found a new treatment that brought him back from the brink of his grim diagnosis. He became strong enough to sit in the saddle of a bicycle and began riding more and more each day. Although he still took regular medications and would for the rest of his life, Barry had completed his first cross-country ride the previous summer with ABB. It took him more than two months to finish, but he did it and in doing so, raised more than $30,000 for his hemophilia organization, Save One Life. Then he decided to do it again on an even tougher route—the Fast America Ride.

As each rider shared his story, I wanted to disappear right into the floor. When my turn came, I stood, stared at my feet, and said, "Hello, my name is Eric," my heart beating so hard beneath my jaw that I was sure everyone could see it. "Um, my dad and I signed up for this ride because I wasn't really sure what I wanted to do after college. When he offered to take me on this trip, I said yes." My introduction felt so lame and insignificant compared with what I'd already heard that my ears burned red with embarrassment. As I sat down, I felt an overwhelming sense of relief that the attention was off of me and on my dad as he stood to speak. I could faintly hear him introducing himself and discussing his reasons for wanting to ride across the country. I knew I should be interested in what he was saying, but his voice and the Starfish Room were slowly fading away and somehow I was back in my junior year of college.

I was no longer in a room full of cyclists listening to stories about being courageous and overcoming odds. I was no longer strong and healthy from months of fitness training and healthy living. Instead, I was exhausted from lack of sleep and so out of shape I didn't recognize myself in a mirror. I was depressed and scared out of my mind. And I was not alone. I was sitting in a church basement on a metal chair so cold I could feel the chill through my jeans. Everyone was sitting in a circle in one of those small, out-of-the-way places where people go to share their struggles with something that has ripped apart their lives and those of the people around them—substance abuse.

The visions came flooding back. A woman sitting across from me quietly cried. I assumed she was older, but I couldn't tell because her face was so ravaged she could have been anywhere from forty to seventy. She was curled up on the seat of her chair as if trying to vanish from reality through sheer force of will. Between sharp, hitching breaths, she told us how she'd lost the will to live after yet another relapse. Her children refused to speak to her. She couldn't pay her rent, and if she got her hands on any more drugs, she knew it would be the last thing she ever did.

The rest of the group nodded in silent understanding while I sat numb and horrified, thinking that none of this had anything to do with me. Surely I must be in the wrong place. And then a man said that he was grateful to the group for its support because for the first time in a long time, he didn't cringe when the sun came up and draw the curtains on a new day—another day of trying desperately to be better, to find his old self, and to make his family and friends proud, only to feel he was losing the battle with drugs and alcohol. *Okay,* I thought, *I know that feeling.* How many times had I drawn my own curtains against the light? How many times had I locked my door while my confused friends shook their heads on the other side? Sadly it was too many times to count. Maybe this meeting had something to do with me after all.

The vision changed again. I was sitting in a small classroom filled with young people. We were all at desks, arranged in a square. A girl, close to my age, was telling the group about a recent afternoon when she sat in her apartment with all the lights turned off because after she bought drugs, she'd had no money left to pay utility bills. The only light in the room was the flickering of her lighter; the only thing she could see was the metallic reflection of the spoon in her hand.

Our counselor asked her if there was anyone she could rely on to help her stay clean. She replied that the only people she knew were the kind who would jump off of a roof to get the painkillers to which they were so horribly addicted. She recalled how her ex-boyfriend had smashed her head into the windshield of a car for no apparent reason when he was high on meth. She cried when she told us that she just wanted to get her daughter back and to raise her right after finally getting clean. Next, a pale young man talked about how he had overdosed on pain medication. His wife found him lying next to her in the morning, his lips blue and his hands cold to the touch when she tried to shake him awake.

Then it was my turn. "Hello, my name is Eric. I'm an addict." Those words would always be bitter in my mouth. Every time I had to say them during my months in treatment, I'd look around at the other people in the group and never fully make the connection with what it meant to be an addict. It was difficult for me to fathom their lives. My weed dealer had not almost beaten me to death in front of my friends. I hadn't lost the mortgage payment or allowed my lights to be shut off because I spent all my cash on hard drugs. I hadn't lost a child to protective services. I wasn't addicted to painkillers, cocaine, or meth—yet. When I heard about their pain, destruction, sadness, anger, guilt, and regret, the only thing I felt was a sense of relief that my life hadn't gone that far off course.

However, through the months of substance abuse classes and NA meetings, I became painfully aware that if I hadn't made a phone call to my mother on an early March morning, finally admitting to her that I was lost, scared, and needed help, chances are I would have ended up sitting in that room telling strangers about the terrible things that I had done or that had been done to me—or worse. I had gotten to such a desperate place that I began contemplating harder, more dangerous drugs to silence the voices that wouldn't stop telling me something in my life was horribly wrong.

Instead of speaking up in college about how confused, depressed, and scared I was becoming, I let everyone think I was still the same friendly, carefree E-Wags, my nickname since middle school. When pretending to be happy became too difficult, and I couldn't bear the thought of my parents, friends, and teachers knowing the real me, I'd numb myself with drugs and alcohol and hide in my room for days.

When I finally got up the courage to try to get on the right path again, I'd strap on a huge smile, make mile-long to-do lists, run six miles on shaky but determined legs, call my parents to tell them how great I was doing, go to class, and promise myself I'd stay in the library for as long as it took to catch up on the previous week's ignored work. It doesn't take a genius to know how that strategy worked out. As soon as it became painfully obvious how deep a hole I'd dug for myself, I drew the shades and locked the door again. Patrick, my roommate and one of my best friends since elementary school, looked at me day after day with concern and confusion in his eyes. I could see him wonder what had happened to the confident, self-assured Eric he'd known back in high school and at the beginning of college.

I wondered too. I wondered every day and wanted desperately to become that young man again. I wanted to turn back the clock to the time in my life when the word *limitation* didn't exist in my vocabulary, to feel the passion that used to fill me when I chased my dream of being a writer. Somehow all of that had fallen by the wayside as alcohol and marijuana became the numbing focus of my life because I couldn't face the hard questions when things started unraveling.

When we first met, I had attempted to convince my substance abuse counselor, Kelly, that I didn't belong there, but he had sternly replied, "Yes, Eric, you do. You are addicted to something that is ruling and ruining your life whether you want to believe it or not." He hadn't been the kindest or gentlest person during those months, but he wasn't supposed to be. He wasn't my friend or my buddy; he was my substance abuse counselor, and it was his job to help me move past my mistakes, regain control of my life, and learn how to avoid ending up there again.

When I finished the program, he had shaken my hand and told me he wished there were more people like me. He said that I was a rare breed of person and that he was proud of me. I'd been confused by his compliments because despite making it through the program, I still had a pretty low opinion of myself. I felt I'd done a fantastic job of screwing up my life and my values.

Until the afternoon of our ABB orientation, most of those

difficult memories had been locked tightly away in another part of my mind. During the months of training, I'd tried not to dwell on the past too much. Instead, I focused on how many miles I was riding that day and what route I would take along the roads of New Jersey. But with that introduction to the group of cyclists—"Hello, my name is Eric"—I was right back at each meeting, listening to every last painful and humiliating story.

Somehow I forced myself back to the Starfish Room. Mike wrapped up the meeting, and slowly my inner turmoil faded. Once again I stuffed the bitter memories back into the closed parts of my mind, but something told me that I was putting a temporary bandage on an open wound. At some point during this ride I knew I would have to deal with these unresolved feelings; I just wasn't ready yet. The question of where and when it would happen scared me to death.

Most of the group decided to get together for dinner at an Outback Steakhouse before the ride began the next day. I quickly returned to our room to change, and my dad, sensing my quiet demeanor, asked if everything was okay. I was still shaken by my thoughts but was determined to act as if everything was fine. I brushed him off with a weak smile and a nod. During our walk to the restaurant, I strolled next to Floris, one of my new teammates, who lived in Amsterdam. During my sophomore year in college, I stayed there in a hostel with my brother for five days. I focused on talking with Floris about his beautiful city's canals and architecture. I told him how much I liked the houseboats that floated gently with the ripples of the passing gondolas and admired how the bridges rose so elegantly over each body of water. He told me that he was riding to raise money for War Child, a charity that empowers children and young people in conflict areas.

At dinner I sat next to George, whose vast knowledge of cycling was apparent as he dropped phrases like "lactate threshold," "power output," and "bonking." I tried for about three seconds to pretend I knew what he was talking about, but when he asked me about my personal threshold, I sheepishly admitted I had no idea what that meant. I braced myself for rolling eyes and a disgusted reply about my having the audacity to undertake this ride with so little knowledge. Instead, George smiled and cheerfully explained each phrase. Savoring his chirpy British accent, I soaked up everything he had to offer.

"Threshold is the amount of lactic acid that builds up in your muscles before they are overcome with exhaustion and seize up," he said. "Power output is the amount of force your legs generate against the pedals. There's a device you can attach to your bike that can accurately measure it. Bonking is the equivalent of 'hitting the wall' for marathon runners. It's when your blood sugar tanks and suddenly you have no more energy." George could not have been more patient with his explanations, and I was thankful not to be pretending anymore. More than most, I knew how exhausting pretending could be.

That night as my dad and I gathered our cycling equipment for the next morning, I thought about everything that had happened that day. After returning to the road with Shiva, getting to know the other guys and their unique personalities, and finally cracking open some of my own feelings, riding across the country didn't seem quite so daunting. Maybe that was the point of this ride—to prove to myself and to everyone else that I had what it took to reclaim the life I once loved and to restore the values I once held so dear. Maybe I wasn't the only one with demons lurking or struggles to overcome. Just look at Barry's story.

One thing I had definitely learned in the past few years was that everyone needs help sometime in life. Not asking for help is what got me into so much trouble in the first place, and I was determined never to make the same mistake again. Who cared if I didn't know squat about power output or bonking? I was going to watch, to ask, to learn, and to ride my way across the United States if it was the last thing I did.

Every Journey Has a Beginning

Sunday, April 21, 2013—Morning

IT WAS STILL DARK OUT WHEN I OPENED MY EYES, AND FOR A MOMENT, I couldn't recall where I was as I looked around the unfamiliar room. Then all at once, reality came crashing back: this was the day my father and I would begin our bicycle ride across the United States. Finally, the waiting was over! Adrenaline surged through my body as I quickly sat up. My dad must have woken before me, because a faint light shone beneath the closed bathroom door and the spray of the shower was the only sound in the room. I swung my legs onto the floor, stretching my arms above my head. Mike Munk's advice during orientation was still fresh in my mind. As our bodies adjusted to the sudden increased mileage on the road, it was important to carefully pace each day. If we didn't, we risked injury, and the last thing I wanted was to be sidelined. But after staying off the road for more than a week, with only a short ride the previous day, I was full of energy.

I grabbed all four of the water bottles we'd left next to the sink the night before. They were specially designed with insulation that had kept our drinks cold during long, hot training rides. Each had a twistable nozzle to help prevent spills and could hold up to thirty-two ounces of liquid. We'd been using them since we started training and had dropped them on the road or in the bushes so many times I could easily tell mine apart from my father's. I knew every scrape, dent, and blemish. They were critical to our success because without proper hydration, I doubted we'd make it the first twenty miles.

Before leaving New Jersey I had ordered a special product for us from Gatorade called Endurance. It contains extra doses of sodium and potassium to help prevent cramps during long bouts of endurance training. I took the lime-green powder from my bag and scooped generous portions into each bottle before carefully tightening the caps. When I finished with the water bottles, I felt a little bit better about the day. Once we left our motel room whatever happened on the road would happen, but at least I had control over this one thing. It also felt good to do something for my father that would help him on his journey.

Then I took out my secret hydration weapon—my blue CamelBak backpack with a pouch specially designed to fit snuggly around my shoulders. It looked like a child's toy on my broad back, but I was more than willing to sacrifice looking cool on the bike for the security of the extra water the CamelBak would provide. A tube connected the water bladder inside the pouch to a nozzle in front of my face. It stuck out like a big straw with a clip that secured it at the perfect angle for drinking. Carrying 128 ounces of extra water might have felt like overkill, but I didn't know how much we'd need and I sure didn't want to take any chances. My motto was better to be overprepared than underprepared.

I looked at our bikes, propped up against the air conditioner. It was one of those old-fashioned units that drone loudly throughout the night but never quite achieve the right temperature. I walked over to Shiva and felt cold gusts streaming from the plastic vents. With a shiver, I switched off the unit and ran a hand along Shiva's aluminum frame. It was ice cold, as was my cycling jersey draped across her. Everyone would be wearing his new ABB jersey the first day, and for inspiration, I'd left mine out so I could see it.

After sliding my two water bottles into the holders beneath Shiva's seat, I grabbed my clothes and laid them across the unmade bed. The jersey still felt soft and new, but by the end of the day the silky clean texture would be dampened and stained with hours of sweat. I paused for a moment before pulling the jersey over my head. I'd never do this for the first time again, and I wanted to acknowledge how far I'd come to get here. It felt a bit tight around my arms and my chest, but in the time it took to pop my head through the hole I'd been transformed from an amateur cyclist to a member of the ABB team.

I finished dressing and turned my attention back to packing our gear and our snacks. My dad and I hadn't been sure about the kinds of food provided along the route at the Support Aid Group (SAG) stops that also offered bicycle maintenance and emergency medical attention. During orientation, Barbara had showed us exactly what an ABB SAG stop looked like and gently but firmly explained the importance of washing our hands before digging into any snacks. "One of the most important things on this ride is staying healthy," she'd said. "Nothing spreads germs faster than not properly washing your hands. Right after you sign in, you need to make sure to use either one of these." She motioned to the hand wipes and the sanitizing gel. Just like her husband, Mike, it was obvious Barbara ran a tight ship.

I finished tugging on my cycling shorts and filled my pockets with the supplies we'd packed in our luggage. We had CLIF Energy Bars, CLIF Energy Chews, CLIF Protein Bars, and my personal favorite, little packets of GU Energy Gel, all courtesy of my mother's tireless shopping. I took what I thought would be enough for both of us during our first hundred-plus miles and dumped it all on the bed in a large pile. My dad consumed far less food than I did on our bike rides, so I divided the snacks two-thirds to one-third.

Sorting through them, I reminded myself not to push too hard on our first day. I kept repeating the mantra "Just finish, just finish." Although it would be great to lead the pack, I realized that despite my youth and my eagerness, other members of this group had far more experience. Finishing each day from start to finish was all that mattered, and I was willing to take it as slow as possible to achieve that goal. I knew my dad felt the same way, and we had an agreement to ride toward the back of the pack the first few days. We had a week of riding and more than eight hundred miles of road to cover before our first rest day in Albuquerque, New Mexico.

The shower squeaked off, and my father, wrapped in a towel, emerged from the bathroom in a cloud of steam. "Did you already fill my water bottles?" he asked with a smile. I nodded and continued packing. As dawn struggled to climb over the dark horizon, we were on our way to the parking lot to load our luggage. I realized once again how well Mike Munk ran the ABB program: several fail-safe procedures ensured nobody's luggage (or nobody) was left behind. The parking lot was a hive of activity as twenty-three men in cycling gear hauled their luggage into the open blue trailer. After loading our bags, I signed the hanging clipboard just as Mike had directed and saw my dad's signature next to mine. I felt a surge of pride. I couldn't imagine embarking on this journey without him; just seeing his signature gave me strength.

Once our bags were stowed safely in the trailer, we made our way to the Starfish Room for the last time. The room was a sea of red jerseys, and there was enough spandex and tight-fitting clothing to get us into any nightclub! Riders were busy filling up paper plates from several aluminum trays, and because the chairs hadn't been moved since our orientation the day before, many men were sitting in small groups with paper plates balanced on their strong legs. Others gathered around a small round table covered with sweating pitchers of orange juice. The mouth-watering scents of bacon and fresh coffee filled the room. There wasn't much conversation as everyone ate, but I could see we all had the same unspoken questions: *How will we ride together as a group? Who will be the fastest riders and who will be the slowest? Will everyone get along on the road or will there be bravado and showboating?*

I loaded up my plate with home fries and added a generous amount of hot sauce to my powdered eggs. I silently ate my breakfast, hoping my father and I would not discover the hard way that we weren't cut out to ride with this group. My biggest fear was that we hadn't trained hard or long enough to prepare for what we were about to endure. I didn't know enough about these men to gauge the egos they might be carrying along with their water bottles. If we couldn't keep up, would they ask us to leave? The thought was unbearable, so I quickly pushed it out of my head. I wanted to embrace this moment, not ruin it with questions that I couldn't possibly answer. After all, it was our first day on an epic cross-country journey as father and son. How many people could claim the same thing?

One by one, the Starfish Room emptied as the riders returned to their rooms to retrieve their bikes. I disposed of my paper plate and plastic cup and headed back to our room. In a few minutes I would ceremoniously dip Shiva's back tire into the Pacific Ocean on Newport Beach. Once the celebratory photos were taken and the journey was underway, I had to believe that the hours, days, weeks, and months of intense training would take over as I began pedaling. Shiva and I had only one goal—dipping her front tire into the Atlantic Ocean in thirty-three days. I would take the challenge day by day or sometimes, as I would soon learn, minute by minute.

Leaving It on the Road

Day One: Costa Mesa, California–Palm Springs, California
Distance: 112 Miles
Total: 112 Miles

LEAVING NEWPORT BEACH BEHIND, MY DAD AND I STUCK TOWARD THE very back of the group. The ABB route sheet we were supposed to follow consisted of several pages stapled together, with two columns indicating which turns to take and which roads to follow. All in all, we were looking at a 112-mile trek from Costa Mesa to Palm Springs.

The journey had gotten off to a great start. My dad and I had joined the rest of the riders carrying their bikes down to the shoreline of the Pacific Ocean. The cold surf made my feet tingle as we all smiled up at Mike Munk, standing on a lifeguard stand, taking our picture as we dipped our back tires in the Pacific Ocean. Despite our ride leaders' warning against riding too hard and too fast as well as my own thoughts about proper pacing, I felt pretty cocky. Maybe it was all the adrenaline from the excitement at the beach. Maybe it was because I was young and naïve. Whatever it was, I wanted nothing more than to stretch my legs and to get out in front of everyone else. After eight long months of endless training, my legs had become like tree trunks. I hadn't spent all those hours in the saddle for no reason, and I wanted to show the other riders what a young guy like me could do.

For the first two hours I patiently waited near the back of the group as we rode along side streets and past massive concrete structures that I learned were city water canals. Every now and then, other groups of cyclists would pass us, or we'd come across joggers or the occasional power walker. Near the outer limits of Costa Mesa we rode by large parks with neatly trimmed lawns on each side of us. Children at play shouted, and sports officials blew whistles while monitoring Sunday morning soccer games. Hearing and seeing normal activities on such an extraordinary day in my life seemed somehow odd and out of place. All of my senses felt heightened and I was filled with purpose. Somewhere out there in the vast plains or in the timbered peaks, the questions about my life would finally be answered.

A zealous fire burned within me, and I wanted to stand up in the saddle and sprint to the front. But the sidewalks on which we rode were narrow, and the one-lane bridges that took us over canals kept my dad and me from trying any kind of push ahead. That turned out to be a good thing because after a few hours, I began checking the speedometer on my Garmin. We were going at a strong pace, a little more than I was comfortable with. Sure I was young and fit, but that didn't even slightly compare with the experience and the conditioning of most of these guys.

Like my dad, a few of them were ex-military like Phil from Boston, a former army ranger riding for the Wounded Warrior Project. Some of the other guys worked in corporate settings but had devoted an enormous amount of time to physical fitness. It took me less than three hours riding in the back of the group with my dad to realize that my young age and my bulging biceps didn't amount to much on this trip. The other guys might not have the strength I had in my chest and my arms, but in the world of biking that kind of strength was like bringing a knife to a gunfight.

As I settled into my rear-guard status, my thoughts returned to earlier in the year when my father, my mother, and I had driven to Florida to get ready for my first hundred-mile Century Ride. One night, after training for six hours and eating yet another huge pasta dinner, I sat out on the small patio of our Orlando hotel room with my mother. The only light was the flickering of a candle on our wrought-iron table.

A pen and a pad of paper lay untouched in front of us. For the past hour, we'd been discussing the blog I was going to keep while on the ride. After several unsuccessful attempts at a title, my mother switched gears and pushed a little deeper. An accomplished author and writer, she had a way of getting people to talk about what was under the surface rather than just answering questions. "What is it you like about the bike or riding in general, Eric?" she gently asked me. "How does it make you feel?"

I could see her face outlined in the night. She knew all about my struggles in college, so I felt safe telling her whatever answers came to mind. What would I tell myself if I were to be completely honest about why I liked riding the bike so much? I knew there was much more to riding than feeling good physically about a job well done or about how many miles I covered. While training for the trip, I relished the days when the weather was nice enough to ride outside. I'd put on my cycling gear, lock my shoes into Shiva's pedals, and take her out on the road. I loved that time to myself, and even when my dad and I shared the roads, we didn't talk much, so I usually had just my thoughts for company.

"I like the concept of leaving all of my hang-ups about the past and my worries about the future out on the road," I confessed. "I like leaving behind all of the emotions and voices that keep telling me I can't change my stripes no matter how hard I try. I am free of all of that, free of the pain and the sadness." I paused and looked right at her. "I guess I just like the idea of leaving it on the road." My mother smiled at me, and with that, we both knew we had found our title.

Around midmorning we reached our first SAG stop, and just as Barbara had described, it was well organized. There was a sheet next to a large jug of water where we could sign in with our initials and fill up our water bottles. I dutifully signed my name and hurried over to the bathroom at a nearby fast-food joint. (We had been riding nonstop for a few hours and nature was definitely calling.)

After washing my hands, I splashed water on my face, marveling at its coolness against my flushed skin. I quickly returned to the SAG stop to grab bananas, granola bars, and all kinds of sweet and salty snacks. By the time I finished, many of the other cyclists had already taken off. I was disappointed, but when I walked over to my dad he told me that Barry and Joe wanted to ride with us.

"Absolutely!" I said. "Four is the perfect number." Hurriedly, I clipped my cycling shoes in and followed the three of them out of the stop. Once again I was at the back of the line, but I was content to save my strength. Most of the early morning adrenaline had worn off, and I was still looking at another eighty miles of cycling before we could call it a day. Slowly but steadily, I followed the group as we passed through neighborhoods mixed with huge swaths of orange groves.

I was glad to have filled up my water bottles at the stop because the farther we rode, the higher the temperatures climbed. The sun relentlessly beat down on us. I was sweating freely, but the moisture was sucked into the air because of the dryness of the climate. It was heat like I had never experienced before—dry without even a hint of moisture. Every pedal stroke seemed to leave me panting and dry mouthed while all around me the landscape reflected the dry heat. For every mile we traveled away from the cold waters of the Pacific Ocean, the grass grew coarser and the trees more stunted and bristly. The heat was trying to suck the moisture from my contact lenses, and I was thankful to have my sunglasses. Still, my spirits remained as high as the temperature. I knew that each pedal stroke, no matter how seemingly insignificant, was bringing me that much closer to my goal.

We rode past dirt roads lined with houses and stables. Many properties had fenced-in areas for horses to run free on the red desert soil. From time to time, Joe and Barry pointed out an obstacle or a piece of debris so my father and I could avoid it. Occasionally, someone would call out "Stopping!" or "Slowing!" followed by a signal to the rest of the group. I liked this method of communication because it reminded me of something military officers do during battle. Signals could be given silently and commands enforced among the troops. In many ways, this journey was my battle and these roads my battlefield.

I grew so hot and tired by the afternoon that I decided to stop and rest, telling the others to continue ahead and I would catch up. *Guess I'm not going to show anyone how fast this young guy rides,* I thought wearily. Slumped over my handlebars, I heard a voice call out to me from across the highway. Looking up, I saw a cyclist who wasn't part of our group wave in my direction. "Are you okay?" he asked, looking both ways as he prepared to cross the street toward me. I gave him a thumbs-up. "Yeah, I was just resting," I replied. "Thanks, though!"

The cyclist paused and looked doubtfully past his sunglasses at me. "You sure?" he asked. "You looked pretty beat just now." I nodded so hard that my helmet slid down my sweating forehead. "Yup!" I flashed him a tired smile to emphasize my point. He looked at me with a frown, still unconvinced. "Well, okay then. You shouldn't slump over like that," he said. "People will think you might be dying!"

With that, he turned back in the direction he had come and took off, leaving me alone. *Great,* I thought. *First day on the road and I look like I'm dying!* Wearily, I got back into the saddle and managed to catch up with the rest of the guys at a gas station where they'd stopped to get fresh water and to enjoy the air-conditioning.

After we regained our strength for the next push, we linked up with another rider from the ABB team. His name was Philippe, and when I saw him, my initial thought was, *There is no way this guy is going to finish this ride in one piece.* He was laboring up a hill with sweat pouring down his nose. When he spotted us, though, a large smile split his round face. "Ello," he said in an Israeli accent. "Do you mind if I join you?" My father spoke for all of us and welcomed him to the group. Philippe was a character. He had a beautiful wife, several children, and lots of grandchildren. And much to the dismay of the ABB staff, he liked to ride his bike almost in the middle of the road.

On four occasions that first day, Philippe's tire went flat and we had to spend a collective hour to get him moving again. This tried my patience, especially since we were only halfway through the day, but after each flat tire Philippe apologized and sheepishly thanked us for sticking with him. I couldn't help but smile at his gratitude.

We rode together along a narrow shoulder of the flat, single-lane highway. The desert heat washed over me like a thick blanket I couldn't shake off, and eventually the sands gave way to sharp piles of rocks. It was strange to be able to see so far into the distance, and a couple of times the heat waves created strange images in the desert air. I remembered a cartoon in which a character stranded in the desert is terribly thirsty and overjoyed at the sight of a soda machine, only to get closer and realize it is a cactus. I never quite experienced that phenomenon, but there were definitely times when I could have sworn I saw puddles of water several miles down the highway.

Finally the last leg of the day was in sight, but apparently 112 miles in blistering heat was not quite enough for us. We experienced a slight mishap, or "bonus miles," as Barry liked to call them. We made a wrong turn that led us down a five-mile detour before we discovered we weren't on the right road. I looked back down the way we'd come and realized that for the most part it had been slanted downhill in our favor with the wind gently blowing at our backs.

I said nothing as we turned our bicycles around to face the oncoming wind and to fight the steady incline. After more than one hundred miles on the bike, I didn't care. What was one small hill compared with the whole journey? Barry was upset because he'd been leading us most of the day, and I was quick to let him know that it wasn't his fault, that we all make mistakes. I felt that last part more than most, and he seemed to brighten after my sincere gesture.

Despite being tired, sore, and hotter than I think I'd ever been in my life, my mood couldn't have been better as my dad and I finally pedaled into the motel parking lot. We had finished our first day on the road together and in one piece—with a few bonus miles thrown in for good measure.

The Human Watercooler

Day Two: Palm Springs, California–Blythe, California
Distance: 134 Miles
Total: 246 Miles

WE LEFT THE HOTEL AROUND SEVEN-THIRTY ON A SURPRISINGLY COOL morning. The second day of our journey was underway as I trailed behind my dad through the quiet streets of Palm Springs. It felt odd to be riding with so much civilization around us, because we were still in the middle of a desert and just past the city limits were endless stretches of sand and coarse rock. The city's center, though, reminded me of a setting from a 1950s television show. Palm trees lined litter-free streets. Every home had a well-tended flowerbed, and sprinklers hissed over glistening sod lawns. A sparkling BMW or Mercedes was parked outside most of the gated houses we rode past. I half expected to see a milkman making deliveries from house to house or a paperboy riding his route on a little red bike with a satchel of penny presses tucked neatly in his front basket. With the exception of a few birds singing in the well-kept trees, it was quiet.

The sky was quickly losing its shade of bruised purple as dawn crept past the Little San Bernardino Mountains and light spread along the Coachella Valley floor. Soon the sun would reach past the towering peaks and take back the cool, shaded desert below. Light-sensitive street lamps flickered off as I took another long sip of water and tried not to think about what would happen once that sun hit us on the desert floor. The previous night, Mike had cautioned everyone about the severe heat we'd face the next few days as we rode into the heart of the California desert. I'd been hot and thirsty enough as it was the day before, and the thought of voluntarily going back out in this heat felt insane. In Costa Mesa, it was sunny and in the seventies. But here, half a day's drive from the coast, the temperature was steadily climbing into the triple digits. We never had to deal with anything like this while training on the East Coast, and I nervously wondered how my father and I would fare.

Quickly, I shook off any foreboding thoughts and focused on getting enough to eat and drink and on what time my dad and I needed to report to RAP later that evening. The letters didn't stand for anything in particular but referred to a briefing that "wrapped up" the day. This was a simple enough schedule to keep, and I liked the consistency and the structure it provided. For a moment I imagined what life must be like in New Jersey. *It must be getting close to noon back home*, I thought. *I wonder what everyone's doing right now.* At home there would be no worries about when the next SAG stop would be, if the soaring temperatures might cause heatstroke, or whether I would run out of water. A wave of loneliness struck me as I watched my dad, a few yards in front of me, slowly turning his pedals. He was the only person I really knew for hundreds of miles in every direction.

A quick head count of the riders ahead of me confirmed that well over half the ABB team was sharing the road. I remained as close to the back as possible while the group navigated the streets in single file. With hardly any traffic and no major highways, we felt comfortable enough to ride in a loose formation. I was careful not to get too close to any of the groups. I'd gotten to know a little bit about most of the riders, especially Joe, Max, Jan, Barry, and George, and they all seemed like good-hearted guys. I enjoyed their company, but I wanted to keep the ride simple, preferring not to add too many people to the unpredictability of potholes, wildlife, weather, and careless drivers.

For a while I rode next to Max, the outgoing Australian. Since he was from Down Under, we talked about how much my friend Keira loved living in Australia. "You should bring her along when you come visit," he said. Eventually we got around to talking about life. I listened eagerly because Max seemed like a man who lived a full life, and I wanted to get his perspective on things. "I have to admit I'm a little bit selfish, a little bit greedy," he said. "I want the most out of every day, every hour, because you never know when it might all be over." I told him the only thing I wanted out of life was to live it to the fullest. He smiled and nodded.

Our conversation turned to my college days, and although I didn't admit I'd needed help, I confessed I'd spent too much time partying and not enough time studying, which made me uncertain about my future. "I had a friend once, a longtime friend who was smart as a whip," Max said. "But when drugs came into the picture, she just lost it. I still see her sometimes, but when I talk to her, I can just tell that she's not all there. Drugs can do that to you, mate. They can take the best of you and bring you down to a lower level." He licked his parched lips and went on. "I had a neighbor, one of the nicest blokes you'd ever meet, and he had some of the most incredible dreams. But he never seemed to do anything but smoke weed, and those dreams went up in smoke. He'd just sit around doing nothing all day."

I didn't say anything much after that, but Max and I continued to ride together for a while longer in companionable silence. Sometimes sharing the silence with someone can be just as powerful as an intimate conversation.

I took another sip of water. My dad and I had discussed the importance of knowing when and how much to drink. Once the sun finished climbing over the peaks, there wouldn't be much shade on the road for the rest of the day. We left the city behind and sure enough it didn't take long before the temperature soared. The sky was as clear and blue as the deepest ocean, and I saw no more than two or three small clouds all morning as we rode into the full embrace of the outlying desert.

We pedaled by acres and acres of ordered rows of produce and dense fields of orchards stretching far into the distance on either side of the highway. I was amazed that so much farmland had been cultivated in this dry, arid climate. Irrigation hoses hung over the crops from delicate wires and sprayed fine clouds of refreshing mist over the vegetation. Every time our group would get near a hose, I'd maneuver Shiva so I could get sprayed. It felt amazingly cool for a moment but the feeling never lasted. Almost immediately the desert heat sucked the moisture out of my damp ABB jersey, the same one I'd worn the first day. Though I'd brought three extra jerseys from home, I loved wearing my official jersey. It filled me with a strong sense of pride.

Every few miles, we passed hired hands milling about, waiting for their turn to work. My thoughts turned to one of my favorite books, John Steinbeck's *The Grapes of Wrath*. I imagined the lives of these people, stooped over crops for hours every week for meager pay. It made me sad to see them, and many times that day I looked into the fields with a new appreciation for all of the comforts of life that had been provided for me. I didn't know what it was like to go hungry because I hadn't been chosen to work or what it was like to toil out in the desert heat all day, picking strawberries, lettuce, or whatever crop was in season.

The morning stretched on and the temperature continued to rise. Once we left the farmland behind and reached the true desert outside Palm Springs, my ABB do-rag wasn't even getting damp anymore. Instead, a ring of dried sweat lined the inside of the cloth in a powdery white crust that crumbled away in my hands when I ran a finger over it. I looked down at myself and saw similar rings around the neck and the shoulders of my jersey and across my chest. I shrugged—just one more thing outside of my comfort zone. Heck, by this time I couldn't have picked my comfort zone out of a police lineup.

We'd been riding through the desert for a few hours when I noticed my dad was dropping farther and farther behind. He'd been unusually quiet during breakfast and even more so as we rode through Palm Springs. I hadn't paid too much attention, because

I was so focused on getting through each mile, but now it was difficult not to notice since he rode several yards behind the rest of us. Jan, Max, Joe, and I stopped to wait for him. As he slowly caught up to us, I knew immediately from the look on his face that something wasn't right. He had the grim look of a man fighting for every inch he gained. I asked him if he was feeling all right and he shook his head.

Jan and my father talked quietly for a few minutes and my father confessed to Jan that he was struggling to keep anything in his stomach, including water. Jan immediately flagged down Mike, and they decided to get him to a hospital immediately. Mike put my father's bike in the van's bike rack and quickly drove off with my dad stretched out in the backseat. When Jan told me what was happening, I slowly nodded my head. I was too tired and hot to say anything, and I knew the only thing I could do was keep pedaling to our motel in Blythe. I'd learn more once I arrived. Jan, Max, and Joe kept me company for the rest of the day. It was a kind gesture that I didn't expect from anyone this early in the ride. We were strangers and their act of generosity made me realize what genuine guys they were.

Around one o'clock, just past Joshua Tree National Park, the four of us discovered we were down to our last reserves of water. Then about an hour from our last SAG stop, one of the riders announced he was completely empty. We stopped on the side of the highway to check our water bottles, rocks stretching to infinity on either side of us while a hot wind blew against us with each passing vehicle. It turned out that everyone was out of water except for me, so we carefully divided my water among the group and rode on. Because of my CamelBak and me, the rest of the guys had water to drink and I was proud to be helping my new friends. I resolved then and there never to take it off even on the days when it didn't seem necessary.

By the time the day came to a close, I learned the heat had claimed another rider, David from Minnesota. I wasn't surprised. He'd been one of the faster riders, and since he hailed from such a cold state, was a likely candidate to be affected by the intense heat.

Later in the ride, I remember him proudly announcing one evening that his hometown had received a record amount of snow in May. Clearly he wasn't used to desert heat. *At least my dad will have some company in the emergency room,* I thought. I was surprised more of us hadn't suffered the same fate. A few guys had quit riding at the last SAG stop rather than risk their health, Joe and Max included. Being young and determined, I felt like I could make it the rest of the way, and Jan kept me company during the last stretch. By the time we pulled into the town of Blythe, I was completely exhausted.

When we got to the motel, I was anxious to learn more about my dad's condition. My luggage was one of the few pieces still left in the lobby, and with a sinking heart I immediately spotted my father's too, confirming he hadn't returned from the hospital. I put Shiva and our combined luggage away in our room and went off in search of a staff member. Karen was in a hallway, maneuvering a luggage dolly loaded with empty watercoolers. She told me Barbara would pick up my dad when the hospital called, but she didn't know when he would be released.

Joe, Max, and Jan invited me to join them for dinner at the local restaurant. I felt awkward eating without my dad but gratefully went along. Nervous I would miss his call, I kept checking my phone throughout the meal. They seemed to understand my concern, and conversation was kept polite and brief. Max surprised me when he ordered a beer. I listened with fascination as he discussed different brews with our waiter. After everything we'd gone through on the road, he still had enough strength to order a cold one. I guess they just make them heartier down in Australia.

RAP was held in the motel parking lot under a star-filled desert sky. I was so exhausted that I almost sat on a big dog turd before one of the other riders pointed it out to me. After such a grueling day in the heat, I could do little more than nod my appreciation before sliding just a smidge further away. I looked around at the group, noting everyone's sunburned faces and raccoon eyes. Many riders asked me about my dad and expressed their concern and well wishes. I told them we were still awaiting word from the hospital.

As we went over the route for the next day, I kept glancing toward the street, hoping to catch Barbara or Karen pulling into the parking lot with my dad in tow. I imagined him stepping out of the van with a big, mischievous smile on his face. "No worries! It was just something I ate," he'd say. "I'll be ready to ride tomorrow." But RAP ended and he never came. It wasn't until I was back in my room, getting my cycling gear together, that my cell phone finally rang. "Dad?" I asked. "Are you okay?" Relief filled my body as I heard him speak. "Hey, buddy." His voice sounded clear but quiet over the line. "I'm still at the hospital. They say that I have to take it easy for the next couple of days. But don't worry," he added. "I won't leave you, even if I have to rent a car and drive behind you the rest of the way."

I didn't know what to say. My father had asked me to come on this ride because he knew I hadn't been able to completely shake the challenges I had faced in college. After graduation, I'd reluctantly confessed to him that I doubted my ability to make good choices for my future as a result of making such poor ones in the past. As a military man, my father wanted to put me in a situation where I had to rely only on myself and in doing so, rebuild my confidence. The fact that he might not be able to ride alongside me was a huge blow to us both. I knew he was totally dedicated to his family, but his willingness to stay by my side, no matter how sick he might be, took that dedication to a whole new level.

"Thanks, Dad." It was all I could manage to say.

Tough Comes in Many Colors

Day Three: Blythe, California-Wickenburg, Arizona
Distance: 115 Miles
Total: 361 Miles

MY FIRST WAKING THOUGHT THE NEXT MORNING WAS OF MY FATHER. All night, my dreams had been flooded with endless reels of worst-case scenarios about his stay in the emergency room. I fought the urge to run down the hall and to pound on Jan's door to ask him what he thought had happened on the road the previous day. Was it a ruptured spleen? Severe dehydration? Failed organs? Each thought was wilder than the last, and I started fearing the worst. Regardless of what my dad told me on the phone, would he have to leave the ride and go home? He had trained just as hard as I had all those months, even enduring two bouts of bronchitis and a bad back.

Selfishly, I also feared for the future of my ride without him. Would I be able to do the rest of this journey on my own? Who would I ride with if he were out of the picture? Would I have to pedal all of the way to the Atlantic Ocean by myself? I didn't know the other riders well enough to feel comfortable asking them to "adopt" me, yet the thought of riding solo was overwhelming.

On top of that, the novelty of the ride was starting to wear off, replaced by a weariness that seeped into my muscles and my bones. Instead of starting the day off fueled with adrenaline and ready to jump onto Shiva, I felt sore, stiff, and hungry—always hungry! That

47

morning I had awoken with a rumbling, demanding stomach and went in search of an extra banana. I always had to make sure I ate enough to satisfy my craving for calories while still being mindful of possible cramps down the road from too much food. No matter how hard I tried to space out my snacking and my meals, though, they were never enough.

When I tried to swing my legs out of bed, they were barely flexible enough to allow me to sit upright. Stretching awkwardly from my seated position, I looked over at the bed beside me and a huge smile crossed my face. My father was back! He must have returned from the hospital during the night, and because of my exhaustion, I had slept right through his arrival. The fears of minutes before evaporated, and I gratefully let go of some of the tension crowded between my shoulder blades. *He must be somewhat healthy if the hospital released him,* I thought. But after taking a good look at him as he sat up in bed, I noticed he still didn't look too well.

"So what did the doctors say?" I asked as casually as I could. I was torn between wanting to be sure he was okay and hoping to hear he was cleared to ride. The throbbing in my back and my hamstrings let me know I could use his motivational presence on the road. "Just a stomach bug," he said, getting out of bed and dressing in his street clothes. "Nothing serious. I should be fine in a few days." He was gamely trying to brush off his setback like it was no big deal, but I could tell from his slow movements and deflated demeanor that the news from the doctor wasn't what he'd wanted to hear. Having to sit out the next few days (at the very least) would be hard for him. I knew it wouldn't be great for me either, but I said nothing.

I went through my mental checklist for the day. The routine was getting more streamlined—two water bottles, my trusty CamelBak, Gatorade mix, protein bars, granola bars, GU Energy Gel packets, and a bucket of ice to add to my drinks. I checked over Shiva, looking for any punctures in her tires or wear in her chain. Mike had taught us to use the "spit test" to check for leaks in the tires. If a rider suspects a leak, he spits over the area, and if it bubbles, there's a leak. Thankfully, I hadn't had to spit yet.

My father quietly packed his gear. He was obviously wondering what he'd do with his time off the bike, and the idea wasn't sitting well with him. "Maybe you could take some pictures of me on the road for the blog," I offered. At least that would give him something to do besides stare out the window from the support van as he watched the riders. I thought about which team member I might ride with in place of my dad. It was still too early to know who could ride at what level. There were a few guys going strong in the front whom we'd ultimately nickname the Four Horsemen. I was pretty sure I wouldn't be seeing too much of them. Everyone else was still mingling on the road and getting a feel for different paces. Still mindful of my own pace, I made sure I didn't push too hard for too long. To keep going was a delicate balancing act between body and mind. Sometimes I felt strong, like I could race to the front of the pack and back without breaking a sweat. Then there were times when my legs felt more like two stiff logs than the limbs I needed to push Shiva along.

Based on the past few days, Joe seemed like the best riding companion for me. I liked his personality, his mentality on the bike, and his attitude about the trip and I hoped he'd allow me to ride with him while my dad was sidelined.

I finished packing and headed out of the motel toward the Denny's across the street for breakfast. The huge bowl of oatmeal I ordered helped fortify my energy as I watched the sun break through the cloud-covered horizon. I've always been an early riser, and getting up before the sun rose agreed with me. Even in the sleepy little town of Blythe, California, the new day inspired me.

The desert air had warmed up a few degrees, but it was still cool as we headed out. Judging from the past two mornings, I knew the cool temperatures wouldn't last long. I was acutely aware that my father wasn't with me, but when I saw him barely touch his food at breakfast I was happy he was resting in the van. This wasn't what either of us wanted, but the goal was to let his body recuperate so he could get back in the saddle as soon as he was strong enough. My father knew that sometimes a soldier had to give up a battle to win the war.

My legs became less stiff and sore with each mile, and before I knew it, Joe and I were passing into our second state of the trip—Arizona! At some point, Max and Jan joined us, and the four of us rode together. But as the day wore on and the morning sun beat down on us, I labored to keep up with the three of them. My jersey became covered in dry, flaking sweat, and I made sure to keep sipping water every few minutes to keep moisture in my mouth. All around us, the sun-scorched desert shimmered with waves of rising heat as large tumbleweeds blew across the arid Arizona sands. We stayed together until a few miles before the last SAG stop of the day when I decided I needed to hang back to conserve my strength.

Riding into the stop, I felt dejected and alone until I saw my father waiting for me with a big smile on his face. Despite his illness, he grabbed my water bottles the moment I got off of my bike. What flavor of Gatorade did I want from the water station? How many bananas and what kinds of snacks could he get me for the rest of the day? Here we were, in the middle of the desert, with my father suffering from an awful stomach illness, yet he still projected an image of confidence and reassurance for me. Wearily and gratefully, I allowed him to fuss over me like a mother hen over a chick. I desperately needed his presence, especially with the last leg of the day's journey looking so difficult. My heart felt much lighter as I rode out of the parking lot with my refilled water bottles and my pockets stuffed with healthy snacks.

I got an unexpected surprise an hour down the road when Karen and Mike rode up alongside me. With fresh legs, they were cruising at a 20 mph pace, a bit quicker than my usual 16 to 17 mph. I cranked it up for a while, but my sore legs started cramping in protest against the sudden increase. The two of them were kind enough to slow the pace a little and stayed with me on one of the longest roads of the day. The desert stretched out as far as the eye could see until it curled up against a distant mountain range. That afternoon I saw my first dust devil, a vortex of hot air, sand, and dust swirling around the desert plains. Despite my exhaustion, I couldn't help but marvel at the pristine beauty of the landscape and felt grateful to be seeing it up close from Shiva's saddle.

Karen and Mike had to get going to the motel, so they left me with the promise that I had only a few miles left. Hearing their encouraging words, I felt relieved that soon I would be able to escape the scorching heat to cool down and rest. I'd ridden the farthest I'd ever gone on a bicycle, and even though this had been one of the most grueling days of my life, I let out a triumphant yell. Alone in the desert with nothing more than the buzzards for company, I could hear my voice reverberating across the slate and the sand. "This is the farthest I've ever gone. Woo-hoo!" By the time Shiva and I rolled into Wickenburg, Arizona, I was on top of the world.

My father was waiting for me in the motel lobby. As he followed me up to our room, he said, "Barbara told me that sitting in an ice bath helps with the soreness. You want to try it?" I stripped off my sweat-soaked garments and dropped them on the motel floor. I was up for anything, so I wearily nodded. He smiled and said, "I'm on it! Call your mom and let her know you're alive. I'll get it all ready for you."

I will never forget how my father cared for me that day despite needing someone to care for him. And he didn't just care for me. Because I was the last one to reach the SAG stop that day, I observed him busily gathering up the camping chairs spread out for the other riders, picking up empty paper plates and other bits of trash, and helping out wherever he could. I had no doubt that he had handed out water bottles and snacks to other riders. Beneath the big grins and the warm handshakes, my dad has steel in his personality; you don't get to be an army ranger without it. But in his few days out of the saddle, I learned something just as valuable about his attitude toward life. Leading isn't just about giving orders. It's about pitching in when things get tough and about motivating those around you to be their best. Just because you're down doesn't mean you have to be out.

Tough comes in many colors.

Ain't No Mountain High Enough in New Jersey

Day Four: Wickenburg, Arizona-Cottonwood, Arizona
Distance: 104 Miles
Total: 465 Miles

THE FIRST REAL CLIMBING OF THE TRIP AWAITED US JUST A FEW MILES AWAY from our motel. It would be a true test of my training: tackling more than one hundred miles while climbing eight thousand feet toward our next destination in Cottonwood, Arizona. I'd already ridden farther in three days than on most weeks during my training in New Jersey. There hadn't been many challenging climbs among the hills in the northwest part of the state, certainly nothing like the ride we faced on the fourth day of our journey through Yarnell, Prescott, and up Mingus Mountain. We'd have to fight for every inch climbing up mountains that stood taller than six Empire State Buildings.

Leaving my dad in the support van with Barbara for another day, I rode out with a group of five or six. We'd been riding only a few minutes before we reached the highway and the road cut sharply upward. As I quickly lowered my gears, my stiff muscles struggled against the cold morning and the sudden incline. I was wearing layers against the chill, but I hadn't ridden Shiva long enough to properly warm up. My drowsy mind hadn't fully awakened, and the only sound I heard was my labored breathing over the steady creak of Shiva's bike chain.

I was just starting to feel my legs loosen up when I was almost jolted out of my seat by the sound of an eighteen-wheeler's horn. Since we had left California, there had been times when drivers had honked at us in a courteous, positive way, hanging out of their windows and flashing us the thumbs-up sign or just smiling and waving as they drove by. But this was definitely not a friendly honk! It sounded like the booming horn of a large oil tanker lost in a fog bank. It wasn't even eight in the morning, and it took several terrifying moments for my panic-stricken brain to process what was happening. A massive cab was muscling its way past us on a road with a thin shoulder, and there wasn't much room for us to maneuver.

The truck blew its earth-shattering horn a second time as it overtook us. Several colorful expressions filled the air in its wake as the ABB riders avoided the speeding truck as best they could. Finally the large truck disappeared from sight and silence returned, but the experience left my legs tingling with fresh adrenaline. Apparently not everyone on the road appreciated our mission.

The mountains dominating the horizon were enormous, easily taller than the ones we had seen near Palm Springs. Cars shone brightly in the early morning light as they crawled up numerous switchbacks like tiny metallic ants. Our route flattened out a bit, and I decided to get out of the saddle to shake off the close-call jitters. I pulled off to the side of the road and took out my camera for a quick photo of what I was soon about to tackle. Several riders passed me, and I shouted out brief words of encouragement. We were going to the other side of the mountain range, and I hoped we'd all make it in one piece. Standing alone on the side of the road, I wished my dad could have been with me to share the moment. He would have loved to face off against something this challenging. Today, though, it would be just the mountains and me. I swallowed hard and got back into the saddle.

Shiva and I slowly advanced on the foothills. Drawing closer, I tightened my grip on her worn handlebars, took a deep breath, and dropped her gear down one more time. Most of the guys in the group had wiry, lean upper bodies and powerful legs honed from years of cycling. One glance at me on a bike would be all you'd need to see climbing was not my specialty. I could get away with being top heavy in New Jersey, but that was because there hadn't been challenging climbs. Sure, there had been the occasional hill, but for the most part, the roads near my house were gentle slopes and long, straight flats. I'd never tried climbing something so steep and towering. What if I couldn't get up and over?

I heard George's words ringing in my ears: "These arms, mate! Good for girls but not for cycling!" At the time I'd chalked up his comment to his British humor, but from the moment I began climbing into the foothills I felt every extra ounce of my upper body weight trying to drag me back down the way I'd come.

I quickly left the foothills behind and hit the steeper switchbacks with fierce determination. With each jolting pedal stroke forward, I felt my body as an extension of my will. I was already at the lower end of resistance on my gears, and although part of me knew there was still a great deal of mountain to conquer, I forced myself to focus on the road right in front of my bike. *Get to that point. Good. Now get to that point a little farther up*, I'd whisper over and over to myself. It became a game. Each half turn of Shiva's pedals brought me closer to my next target. I'd focus on another spot just ahead on the road, and the game continued. Again and again I'd play, each time feeling a little victory and an ever-deeper sense of satisfaction that I was literally conquering a mountain.

I looked down below and saw several of my team members fighting the same battle. Arizona stretched out below me like a vast carpet of red sandpaper. The sun-blasted landscape with wind-twisted spires made from ancient rock reminded me of a science fiction movie set on Mars. We continued to climb into the higher reaches of the mountains, and the air became cooler and cooler. As always, my CamelBak was fastened securely on my back. I was grateful I could drink easily from the accessible nozzle draped over my shoulder, because I was afraid that if I took my focus off of the road for even a moment, I would lose control and fall over. The thought of having to get back on my bike on this incline, with no momentum, was impossible to fathom.

More times than I could count we rounded the corner of what I thought (and hoped) might have been the top of the mountain, only to discover it was one of the longest and steepest switchbacks yet. I tried to look at my watch to see how long we had been riding, but my body swerved the instant I took my hand off of Shiva's handlebar. My guess was that we'd been climbing for at least three hours. There was no one else on the road, and I'd been riding with only the constant moan of the wind as my companion.

The view was still impressive, but my thigh muscles and lower back had started to burn with exertion. My pace was painfully slow, and I realized that I was running out of lower gears on Shiva's sprocket. There were moments when Shiva hadn't moved at all and I had balanced precariously on two wheels between pedal strokes. It was all I could do to keep placing one halting pedal in front of the other, bearing my full weight down and pulling up as hard as I could with each stroke. Eventually I began alternating between standing and seated positions to give different muscle groups the breaks they so desperately needed. To make matters worse, the air began to get thinner and colder, and each inhalation smarted against my teeth. Grimly, I hung on to Shiva and continued to work my legs until at last the climb flattened out. I had made it!

When I reached our SAG stop, my dad was waiting for me next to the support van parked in a gravel lot beside a lonely diner. He took my picture at seven thousand feet above sea level before I loaded up with more snacks. I stopped in the diner for a quick bathroom break, and since there were still a few more climbs to face as well as a ten-mile descent, I quickly got back into the saddle.

Coasting down the back of the mountain, I was careful to apply steady pressure to the brakes to prevent an out-of-control descent. At one point my speedometer read approximately 37 mph, faster than I'd ever gone on Shiva. It might have gone even higher, but I didn't spend too much time looking, because I was afraid to take my eyes off of the road for even a second. I applied the brakes again and again to slow Shiva down, making sure to keep spinning her pedals to avoid leg cramps, just as Karen had told us during breakfast that morning. I thought I heard her words of advice in my head before realizing she was shouting them while zooming past me, a blur on her own bike. Within seconds, she rounded the next corner and disappeared from sight. She had obviously done this before!

I arrived at the bottom of the mountain and had only a few miles to go before reaching the motel. I shifted in the saddle uncomfortably. Since getting on Shiva that morning, I had noticed a burning sensation on the inside of my compression shorts where my rear end and the saddle met. I'd never felt such chafing in my life, and it had grown worse with each passing hour. I made it back to the motel just before RAP, so I dropped off Shiva and gingerly made my way to the meeting. Wincing with pain, I hobbled with tiny, awkward steps. I couldn't let my thighs rub together due to the fierce burning accompanying each stride. As I shuffled along, Jim, another ABB rider, joined me and gave me a quick once-over. "Looks like you could use some butt paste," he said in a matter-of-fact tone. I looked at him uncomprehendingly. *There is no way I could have heard that correctly,* I thought. *Paste … for your butt?* "You know, for saddle soreness," he said.

I thought that the words *butt* and *paste* should never appear in the same sentence, but Jim seemed to believe that this had been the most normal thing in the world to say. I followed him to his room where he produced a small, toothpaste-shaped tube with a picture of a baby and the words "Boudreaux's Butt Balm" (known as butt paste among riders) written across the side. I took this concoction from his outstretched hand with a doubtful expression on my face. "Trust me," he said. "Put this on, and you'll be feeling much better." I thanked Jim and slipped the tube into the back pocket of my jersey. I tried to pay attention to Mike during RAP, but all I could think about was Jim's advice and his special help in a tube. Oh man, I hoped it would work!

Give That Man a Cookie

Day Five: Cottonwood, Arizona-Winslow, Arizona
Distance: 107 Miles
Total: 572 Miles

GETTING OUT OF BED THE NEXT MORNING, I DISCOVERED TO MY immense relief that the fire around my backside had been extinguished. Swinging my creaking legs onto the chilly floor, I grimaced at the uncomfortable tightness in my quads and my lower back from the long climb of the previous day. The good news, though, was that my dad was cleared to get out of the van and back into the saddle. I was happy we would be sharing the road again, but I wanted to be sure he didn't push himself too hard. I'd be keeping a sharp eye on him.

Riding out of Cottonwood, we faced the coldest start of the trip. My breath instantly became great pluming clouds of vapor as I pedaled down Highway 89A. On our 107-mile route, we'd pass through Sedona National Park and Old Creek Canyon, heading toward New Mexico. I was excited to see the famous towering sandstone pillars of Sedona. As the early morning hours passed, the road grew steeper and hills appeared more frequently until the muscles in my back and legs protested. After a lengthy stay in the mountains, they were letting me know they'd had enough of steady inclines. It was tiring work, but every time I felt doubt creeping into my mind, I looked at my dad and felt renewed strength. If he could ride up these hills without complaining after what he'd been through, so could I.

For most of the morning, my dad and I shared the road with Big Dan, a nickname I gave to one of our fellow riders the moment I met him. He looked like he'd be more at home on a football field than on a bicycle; his legs appeared powerful enough to bench-press a ton. With a ready smile and a disarmingly soft southern accent, Big Dan was old enough to have a bunch of kids but young enough so that I looked up to him as a big brother.

Before entering Sedona, we had an unofficial SAG stop for homemade snacks at a small Episcopal church that generously opened its doors to the ABB team. Never one to pass up free food, I perked up when the church appeared. The woman who welcomed us was a gracious hostess whose only request was that we leave our cycling cleats at the door so they didn't scratch the polished wooden floors. I quickly complied, happy to free my sore feet.

After washing my hands (Barbara's words were embedded in my brain), I helped myself to a few delicious brownies and lingered inside to enjoy the peace and quiet of the church. I chatted briefly with our hostess while my dad and the rest of the group filled their water bottles. She seemed interested to learn more about the blog I was keeping during the trip and told me that meeting someone riding across the country was one thing, but meeting a father-son duo riding together was very rare. Outside, the temperature climbed higher and higher as morning dissipated. After we topped off our water and thanked her for her gracious hospitality, she wished us all well on our journey.

We pressed into the hills and the curves of Sedona as massive red sandstone formations surrounded us. The air was crisp and fresh with the scent of pine and cedar. Birds taking flight called out gently while a nearby desert stream babbled. Few cars attempted this two-lane road, and the only vehicles we saw were campers and pickups in no particular hurry to get anywhere. As we traveled through Old Creek Canyon, the road grew so narrow that the wild forests and other foliage pressed on us from both sides. At some points in the park the rock walls of the canyon were so close I could have reached out and touched the rough sandstone with one gloved hand.

I recognized plateaus and pillars and all kinds of rock formations I'd learned about in high school. Talk about a real-life geology lesson. Once we reached the national park, Big Dan, Joe, my father, and I made a quick pit stop at a small convenience store on the side of the road. It was a quaint, rustic place resembling a log cabin. In the parking lot, we spoke with two men from the Netherlands driving cross-country in a fiery red Mustang on their way to New Orleans. "Driving in America is simply amazing!" exclaimed one of them in a heavy Dutch accent. "You could drive for hours and hours and never even have to learn a new language."

The more they spoke about their experiences, the prouder I felt to live in the United States. The journalist in me came out, and I asked the pair what they liked most about America. "You don't need passports or visas to get from state to state," one replied. "You can just pick up and move wherever you want, hundreds of miles from where you started." My father and I shared a knowing look and smiled. We appreciated that last comment all too well because we were still more than 260 miles away from our first rest day in Albuquerque, New Mexico.

As I saddled back up, something Mike had said the night before during RAP came back to me: there would be a tough climb toward the end of the park with sharp switchbacks and turns so tight that by the time we made it to the top, we'd easily see the road on four different levels. We would need three miles of climbing to go two hundred yards straight up! Before leaving, I asked the Dutchmen if they had seen the climb. They looked quickly at each other and grimaced. "My friend," one said, "if you are heading the way we just came, I feel quite bad for you indeed!" With a word of thanks and a resigned sigh, we hit the road once again. Whatever was waiting for us past the pines and the canyon, it would be there whether I was ready or not.

Making my way through the rest of the park, I tried to think about what I'd learned so far that could help me surmount this next obstacle. This trip wasn't about speed; it was about patience. Since the beginning of the ride I'd been frustrated at always being the last one to finish each day. Bone-weary, I'd dragged my sorry butt into the parking lot, arriving so late I'd barely have time to make the RAP meeting, let alone shower and get dinner. But those feelings had begun to fade. If I wanted to survive this next climb—and the rest of the trip—I had to let go of lingering frustrations and focus on each new obstacle as it presented itself. If I pushed myself too hard, I could also end up in the emergency room with some incredulous doctor or angry nurse demanding to know why on earth I thought it was a good idea to ride so fast.

When we reached the start of the climb, the sun was still high in the bright sky. Sunshine filtered through the pine trees and spilled onto the road in pools of shimmering light. The three of us stopped at a roadside store to check out the inventory. When we opened the screen door, a bell loudly announced our arrival and a silver-haired, hippie-style woman emerged from the back room. She commented on my cycling gear and offered to sell us some of her homemade chocolate chip cookies. They were wrapped in cellophane and looked to be the size of both my fists beside one another. Big Dan bought two and shoved them in his back jersey pocket.

After what felt like hours fighting our way uphill, we finally reached the top of the mountain. There had been times when the road had grown so steep I didn't think Big Dan was going to make it, but no matter how slowly we trudged up the inclines, he never quit turning those powerful legs. At the top we stopped to rest and to admire the view of Sedona below us. Big Dan pulled his cookies out of his back pocket and offered me a bite of one. I looked at it for a long moment before gently taking it out of his hands. I don't think I'll ever taste a cookie as good as that one. I had earned every bite, and sharing it with Big Dan made it that much more special.

We couldn't stop for too long, because we still had plenty of miles ahead of us. Our SAG lunch would be in Flagstaff, home of Northern Arizona State University. By the time we arrived at the college, Big Dan had parted ways with us, so it was just my father and I riding through the campus.

The skies were still clear and blue, but the mountain wind had picked up, bringing a chilly feel to the air. The taste of warm chocolate chip cookies earlier in the day was a nice memory, but it couldn't quite compete with another one anxiously scratching at the surface. When I saw the first student ambling down the sidewalk, listening to music with headphones securely in place, panic began to squeeze my chest. I felt hot and flushed despite the growing cold.

In my mind, that young man was me as a freshman at JMU, walking down the sidewalk with a cocky, sure-footed step that could seemingly never be budged off of the right track. He had everything in front of him, a whole world of options to discover as he navigated his way through four years of college. He could be anything he wanted to be. No vision was too bold. His college years could be the best of his life, just as everyone had always told him they would be.

And what had I done with mine? Yes, there were wonderful times with family and friends. I took part in tailgate parties, triathlons, sporting events, and social clubs, always with a fierce pride in wearing the JMU purple and gold. But somewhere along the way, instead of becoming the man I dreamed I would be— the compelling writer, the endearing novelist—I had let fear and indecision paralyze me into someone I didn't recognize, someone who locked himself in his room to shut out those who loved and cared about him, because he was too embarrassed at being so lost and confused.

More and more students flooded the sidewalks and the streets until my father and I were forced to slow our pace to a crawl as we carefully steered through the flowing stream of foot traffic. But the last thing I wanted to do was slow down. I couldn't get off that campus, and away from those memories, fast enough.

Standin' on a Corner

Day Six: Winslow, Arizona-Gallup, New Mexico
Distance: 134 Miles
Total: 706 Miles

MY DAD AND I HIT THE ROAD EARLY. IT WAS ANOTHER COLD MORNING, so we were bundled in plenty of layers. But before leaving Winslow, we had a very important stop to make at the corner of Second Street and Kinsley Avenue. Half of that block is dedicated to the Eagles, one of my favorite classic rock bands of all time. A local family had donated the land for the site decades earlier, and it's called Standin' on a Corner Park. The townspeople of Winslow had painted a mural there to commemorate the famous song *Take It Easy*, the opening track to the band's debut album.

When the Eagles broke up in 1980 and a reporter asked if they'd ever get back together, drummer Don Henley famously replied, "When hell freezes over." Fourteen years later on their hit live album *Hell Freezes Over*, front man Glenn Frey began this memorable song with the famous comment, "And here's how it all started." My mother practically wore out that CD when I was growing up. When I was very young, I'd sit in the backseat of her car and sing along to timeless Eagles songs. She says one of her favorite memories is my little voice chiming in on the chorus of "Love Will Keep Us Alive" or "Already Gone." Their music still dominates a large portion of my playlist, and the thought of standing in a park devoted to one of my favorite bands was beyond thrilling.

When we arrived, the first thing I noticed was the ground covered in neatly laid bricks and the large mural the town had painted. The sun was just starting to climb up the seven large letters on the wall in front of me: WINSLOW. A few pieces of art had been erected for public display, including an old-fashioned flatbed Ford parked beside the curb. I unclipped one foot and came to a slow halt. Before I dismounted, Mike Munk cautioned us not to lean our bikes against the shiny red truck. My dad must not have heard the announcement, because he immediately did exactly that. While he was moving his bike with a sheepish expression on his face, Mike's fake outrage filled the quiet morning air and widened the smile already spreading across my face. I carefully placed Shiva beside a metal bench.

Most of the other riders were waiting, shifting from one cleated shoe to the next in an attempt to ward off the chill. We'd been riding as a group for almost a week, and I could match almost every name with a face. I walked around the park, my bike cleats making soft clomping sounds against the red bricks underfoot. Many were inscribed with names of the people who had donated money to fund the maintenance of the park. A statue of a man leaning casually against a lamppost was set in one corner. He held a guitar by its neck with the base resting on one booted foot. A sign above him said, "Standin' on a Corner." *All that's missing is the girl in a flatbed Ford slowin' down to take a look at all of these guys in their spandex*, I thought.

The last riders arrived and Mike quickly herded us into position for a group photo. After it was taken, a few of us stayed behind to shoot our own pictures. My dad and I had one of the guys take a snapshot of the two of us standing on either side of the lamppost. The moment I heard the camera click, I knew this was a photo I'd save forever, especially for my mother, who brought amazing music into my life at such a young age. I wished she could have been there to share the moment. I spent about fifteen minutes standing on that famous corner. Finally saying our good-byes to the Eagles and to

Winslow, my father and I got back on our bikes and followed the rest of the ABB team out of town to begin the first of two back-to-back 130-mile days. By nightfall, we'd be in our third state: New Mexico.

I felt happy riding into the desert. The land was flat for miles and I saw enormous plateaus on the horizon. They weren't as close and as awe-inspiring as what we'd seen the previous day, but they were still impressive. I also felt happy because my dad seemed to be holding up well after his illness. When we linked up with a few of the other riders on our way out of town, he didn't complain when everyone picked up the pace.

I rode alongside Big Dan, who talked about his family in Georgia. When he told me he'd recently taken his three children to see the latest *Iron Man* film, I eagerly jumped into the conversation. Growing up, I'd loved to read the Avengers and the X-Men comics, and I was thrilled with the progress being made to put the concepts on the big screen. Our conversation allowed me to take a little mental vacation from my aching muscles. After what I had gone through in Sedona, I didn't know if my legs could take any more serious punishment for a while.

At some point that morning, someone suggested we ride in a pace line to conserve our energy. In such a line, everyone rides single file and the person in the lead controls the pace while the other cyclists stay as close to one another as possible. A proper pace line can significantly reduce a rider's energy expenditure. When you're riding closely behind others, they're taking the brunt of any headwind, allowing you to save energy. After a certain distance or time, the lead rider drops back and the next person takes the lead. There was just one problem: I had never ridden in a pace line. I'd once followed my dad during a particularly windy training ride, but even then, I'd barely gotten near him because I was afraid I might accidentally run him off the road with one careless action. Now I was about to ride in the middle of a pace line with little more than a few inches between my front wheel and someone's rear wheel, moving steadily at more than 20 mph on the shoulder of a major highway. *Oh sure*, I thought. *Piece of cake.*

Big Dan must have noticed my apprehension. "The most important thing about a pace line is communication," he explained. "If nobody around you can hear what you're saying, the whole line is in trouble. We're moving so close together at such fast speeds that if you yell 'Stop!' and no one notices, the whole group is at risk." Still unsure, I peppered him with questions: How do I know how fast to ride in the front? Do you peel off to the left of the group so that others can overtake you on the right? What kind of signals do I need to give the rest of the group and how often?

We spent the next few minutes talking about the proper techniques in a pace line. Big Dan's easygoing explanations calmed me a bit, but I still had my reservations. There was little traffic on the road, and with the exception of our creaking bike chains, the quiet was absolute. I tried to relax by listening to the rhythm of the bike chains. To me, the steady metallic clicking had become a comfort, much like the way mothers rock their infants to sleep near the soothing repetitive whooshing of a dishwasher.

Eventually, we drew together along the road, and the rear wheel of the rider ahead of me inched closer to my front tire. I still felt nervous about navigating the road at such high speeds while riding so close together, but at least my dad was right behind me. As always, his presence helped ease the tension I was feeling. The minute I was snuggly behind the bike in front of me, I felt a huge difference. With the head of the pack taking the brunt of the wind, we were moving at a faster pace than I was used to, but we were maintaining it with far less exertion. I even looked up to check if we were on the same road. I still heard the wind, but it had grown quieter, dropping from a moan to a mere whisper. The resistance against my pedals also dropped, and I carefully switched Shiva's gears so I could keep the proper pace.

The longer we rode the more I settled into the pace line. I was even able to keep one eye on my front wheel while occasionally glancing at the steadily shifting scenery. Tumbleweeds and cacti whipped past us and disappeared into the desert as we made our way across the last few miles of Arizona. With each lead rider who peeled off to the back of the line, I moved up closer to the front, and it wasn't long before it was my turn to lead. The rider ahead of me moved aside, and I eagerly surged forward to the front.

The sudden wind was fresh and cool against my hot face. For a moment I swerved against the resistance of the wind before regaining Shiva's balance and my composure. I felt the presence of every other rider at my back, and even though I couldn't see him, I knew my father was behind me, grinning from ear to ear. It was one of the proudest moments of my life as I led my ABB teammates safely down the road toward Gallup, New Mexico.

Black Hats / White Hats

Day Seven: Gallup, New Mexico-Albuquerque, New Mexico
Distance: 136 Miles
Total: 842 Miles

I DESPERATELY NEEDED A REST DAY. I WANTED TO GET OFF OF SHIVA AND not have to worry about the searing sun, what kinds of terrain the next hour would bring, or if I had enough water to last me for the next twenty miles. And the aggressively worded sign from a day earlier, "Trespassers Will Be Shot," sure hadn't given me a warm, cozy feeling while riding down the road. Visions of air-conditioned rooms, sleeping past dawn, and heated Jacuzzis danced tantalizingly in my head.

I was disappointed to be so exhausted and, by extension, so oblivious to the rugged beauty of the desert. One of my favorite English classes in college focused on western literature about cowboys and Indians. My professor had an almost reverent way of talking about the books we read, such as Cormac McCarthy's *Cities of the Plain* and Owen Wister's *The Virginian*. I loved the stories about tough-as-nails cowboys fighting to protect what was right in a lawless land. We also watched and discussed movies, including *High Noon*, the ultimate summary of the Old West culture: a small-town sheriff, with the odds stacked against him, decides to do the right thing even if it costs him his life. In each story, there was always a clear separation between wrong and right, good versus evil. The sheriffs wore white hats and the bandits wore black hats.

If only real life could have been that simple—a right choice, a wrong choice. Too often in the past few years, I'd felt I'd made wrong choices. But what I'd failed to realize back then was that life is not always black and white; many shades of gray must be taken into account. Up until my junior year in college, I never thought that I'd be anything but successful. All I'd ever wanted was to do the right thing for my writing career, my family, and my friends.

After my frantic phone call, my mother took me to a nearby hotel when she arrived in Harrisonburg. She wanted to talk in a private place away from my roommates so she could get a clear picture of what was going on. I sat on the edge of the bed, shuddering, sobbing, and whispering to her over and over, "I'm not a bad person. I'm not a bad person." At the core of my soul I believed I was a good person with good intentions. But somewhere along the line I'd embraced a life of sadness and apathy with only mind-numbing solutions in a bottle or a joint. I was so self-absorbed that I showed zero regard for the feelings of those closest to me, and I felt more worthless than the dirt I imagined they'd use to throw over my coffin when I was gone.

"Eric, you are still a good person, one of the best I've ever known," my mother said. "You've lost your way, Son. Right now the only thing your father and I care about is you and that you had the courage to admit you are in trouble. Everyone needs help sometime in life, and I'm grateful you called us. Even though we may not know all of the answers right now, we'll find them together."

"What if I have to drop out of college? You and Dad have worked so hard to keep me here. You must be so disappointed in me," I said, sobbing.

"Let's cross that bridge when we get to it," she replied. "You're exhausted right now and need to get some rest. We'll start making phone calls in the morning, but believe me when I tell you that you're not the first college student to hit a rough patch. I'm sure your professors want the best for you, and I guarantee they'll work with you as long as we let them know what's going on. All I ask is that from this moment on you will be honest with me. No more pretending. No more hiding, okay?"

It was one of the hardest things I'd ever admitted, but I was relieved that my lies were finally out in the open. I thought there might be a chance for me after all.

The whole time I rode to Albuquerque, New Mexico, my thoughts kept returning to that morning and the conflict between white and black. For so long, I kept trying to push myself back into the world of white hats where I had comfortably lived most of my life. On the outside, I smiled to the world. On the inside, I was slowly but steadily tearing myself into two sharply contrasting men—the Eric I showed the world and the Eric who lived in the quiet spaces between my darkening thoughts. Everyone knew White Hat Eric. He was the guy from a great family who loved him and was a friend to everyone. He signed up for triathlons and was the life of the party. Nobody knew Black Hat Eric. He was the guy who was scared to death because his future wasn't turning out remotely close to what he'd imagined and he couldn't figure out why.

Black Hat Eric waited for breaks in his resolve as an inner voice whispered, *You've had a tough day. Look at all the hard work you've been doing. Go ahead. Have a drink. Smoke a joint. What's the worst that could happen? Have a few more and then a few more. Now I've got you! You're such a loser. How could you do this to your family? Nobody will ever want to read anything you write. Shut the door. You don't deserve the friends who are knocking. Just ignore them and they'll go away.*

I even heard the voice when I was pedaling on the road. *You can't get your life back on track. You can't finish this ride. You can't outrun your demons. Can't, can't, can't. You're weak. You'll always be a failure. This is just temporary, and the real laugh will be when you decide to quit. I know you'll quit. And then everyone will see what a true loser you were and still are. It's only a matter of time.*

As the day wore on, my thoughts grew as heavy as my body felt. My helmet, made of sturdy plastic and nylon, felt like it had turned into lead. Thankfully, there weren't many difficult climbs, just a few gentle, sloping hills. I tried as hard as I could to keep my mind away from the past and instead dreamed of a hot shower and a bed filled with soft pillows where I would get the rest my mind and my body craved.

Somehow in my wandering thoughts of black hats and white hats, I lost the rest of the group and found myself alone the last ten miles of the day. When I saw an ABB van parked on the side of the street with our mechanic Jim in the driver's seat, my heart leapt. I quickly made my way over to it.

"Hey, Jim!" I said, waving. "Is my dad with the rest of the group?"

"Joe got a flat tire," he explained. "They're about fifteen minutes behind." Jim leaned out of the van, sporting the same "raccoon" tan that I had. "Make sure you keep your eyes open once you get into town. There's a lot of traffic down there." Relieved that I was headed in the right direction, I nodded and thanked Jim. He was right about the traffic because as soon as I coasted into Albuquerque there were stoplights and fast-moving cars everywhere. One angry driver honked at me, but by this time I was getting used to that. I became nervous at one point when I wasn't entirely sure I'd taken a correct turn. I consulted the map app on my phone and saw the hotel as a red pin and Shiva as a pulsing blue dot. I pulled over to the side of the road to better read the street names and quickly became aware of how strange I must look to people, particularly to a large group of Spanish guys hanging out near their muscle cars a few yards away.

This was one of the first times I'd navigated a busy city by myself, and I was forced to keep my head clear and to stay calm despite extreme exhaustion. I wanted to curl up under an overpass and go to sleep, but I knew I needed to stay focused. Settling on a route, I pedaled along and a few miles later caught up with Barry. He was also riding alone and asked me where my father was. "He'll turn up in a bit," I said. "He and Joe had some tire trouble."

Even with the day's difficult memories, when Barry and I pulled into the Marriott parking lot, I felt extremely proud of myself for finishing the first seven days of our ride. Within minutes, Joe showed up with my father in tow, which sent my spirits soaring. At last, our rest day was here. Somebody show me to my bed!

My mom, Lisa, by my side on freshman move-in day at JMU.

My father and I spent countless hours training in our basement.

Getting ready for my first 100-mile ride in Florida.

We were always hydrated and fed thanks to
my mom's endless shopping trips.

The king of multi-tasking fitting in a conference
call with 70 more training miles to go.

It's official!

My first glimpse of the ABB trailer. Little did I know
how much that moment would mean to me.

Our fearless ABB leaders. Left to right: Karen, Barbara, Mike, and Jim.

My faithful companion, Shiva.

A typical SAG stop.

Dipping our back tires in the Pacific Ocean. Only 3,400 miles to go!

Philippe's fourth flat tire on our very first day.

Me in the back sporting my Camelbak
through the deserts of California.

After my father's visit to the hospital, Joe didn't
hesitate to take me under his wing.

Even off of the bike, my father remains upbeat.

He's back!

We're going over THAT??

A music lover's dream comes true.

Midwest

Life is like riding a bicycle. To keep your
balance, you must keep moving.

—Albert Einstein

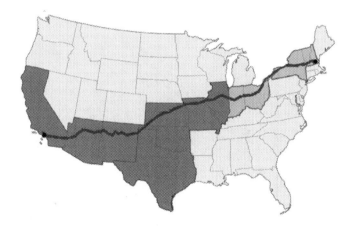

No Man Left Behind

Day Nine: Albuquerque, New Mexico-Las Vegas,
New Mexico
Distance: 137 Miles
Total: 979 Miles

OUR REST DAY HAD GONE BY IN THE BLINK OF AN EYE. SADDLING UP for our ride out of Albuquerque, I felt as if I hadn't moved my legs in a year. With every move I made, no matter how small, my muscles demanded that I head back into the steaming water of the whirlpool bath or to the queen-size bed where I'd spent most of the day watching movies and sitcoms. Instead of going out for a short ride to keep my legs loose, as Mike had strongly suggested, I'd done the exact opposite. After seven grueling days on the road, I couldn't bring myself to get back onto Shiva on my precious day off, so a few halfhearted stretches between meals had been the extent of my physical exertion.

Now I cursed myself for not taking Mike's advice more seriously as I stiffly turned Shiva's pedals through the empty streets of the city into the Sandia Mountains. As usual, it didn't take long for the rest of the group to pull quickly out of sight, leaving my dad and me to navigate the route's turns and stops on our own. At one point we missed a street and had to double back, which certainly didn't improve my cranky mood.

The city awakened and soon I was overwhelmed by the noise

and the commotion. After days of riding along deserted back roads, I felt assaulted by whistle-blowing crossing guards, cars on every corner, and stoplights at every intersection. As I lumbered up the outlying hills, my breathing grew labored and my legs burned with residual lactic acid buildup.

I struggled with the fact that I was about to face one of the longest distances of this journey and some of the most difficult climbs since leaving Arizona. So far on the trip I'd become familiar with doubt, anxiety, elation, fatigue, and fear. But that morning I was just plain angry. After two grueling, back-to-back 130-mile days on the road with only one rest day, we were tackling another 130-mile day of riding, including eight thousand feet of climbing thrown in for good measure. *Are they trying to kill us? What sick mind has concocted this insane route?* I wondered. The past week had been incredibly difficult, but this seemed borderline cruel-and-unusual punishment.

In my muddled and exhausted brain, Mike, Karen, Jim, and even sweet Barbara were all to blame. But I had to admit that I was angrier with myself than with anyone else. I hadn't listened to the wisdom of our ride leader, who had years and years of cycling experience as opposed to my whopping eight days on the road. With twenty-two years behind me, I felt I knew more about my body than he did, and now I was paying the price. It was nobody's fault but my own.

I fought to keep up with the already slow pace my father had set for us. I willed my leg muscles to loosen up just a fraction to offer my pain-racked lower body—a mass of knotted muscles and ligaments—a tiny bit of relief. I didn't begin to loosen up until we were far past the city limits and well on our way along State Road 14. From high up in the Sandia Mountains, Albuquerque looked like a miniature toy set with tiny cars and people moving up and down its streets. It was difficult to imagine people still going about their lives when I was so disconnected from my own. How odd that the Earth was still turning on its axis and that life went on as usual.

A massive slope loomed ahead of me. *If I can just get through this day*, I thought, *I can take on anything the rest of this demanding bike ride has in store.* But the question remained: could I get through the day? Doubts cranked themselves up from a nagging whisper to a relentless roar that grew louder with every aching mile. Each fresh incline sent waves of pain through my screaming quads and aching lower back as we rode higher and higher into the mountains. At some point, my dad went ahead with Philippe while I stayed behind with Joe. It's difficult to gauge exactly when we separated, because my mind was so focused on my faltering will to keep pushing forward. All I knew was that one minute my dad was with me, and the next it was just Joe pedaling in front of me.

The two of us had grown closer the past few days, and I felt lucky to have him for company. He, too, was struggling to maintain his cadence. We tried to keep each other motivated with breathless words of encouragement, all the while dropping into what he liked to call "the granny gear"—the lowest possible one that can be used while climbing a hill. Despite the easier resistance (not to mention the extra gear I had on Shiva's front derailleur that allowed me to drop even lower than the granny gear), I wouldn't have accepted a million dollars to move one bit faster than the pace I was already trying to maintain.

On my first day of tough climbing back in Arizona, I used mental games and tricks to help motivate me up each hill. It had been all about getting to the next point, and the next, and the next until eventually I was at the top. But I was too exhausted, physically and mentally, to fool my brain into playing any games this day. My thoughts were slow and sluggish, and it was all I could do to focus on Joe's rear wheel. Each time I wanted to give up, I brought my eyes back to his steady upward pace while listening to the methodical turn of our pedals.

By midmorning, the temperature was climbing higher, and I knew I would have to dig deeper than I ever had to make it through the day. Thankfully I started seeing signs for Santa Fe where our SAG lunch would be served. Despite the encouraging signs, my legs and back continued to tighten, so I tried different positions to ease the pain. I stood in the saddle, bent far over the handlebars, and stretched my arms high over my head, all to no avail. *Just get me to the SAG lunch so I can properly stretch*, I thought.

After what seemed an eternity of relentless riding, Joe finally spotted the Sante Fe exit and we carefully navigated our way off of the highway. It's amazing how fast cars and trucks can sneak up on you when you're going less than 20 mph and they're doing more than 60 mph. Even when you think you have all the time in the world to cross the exit lane or to follow it off the highway with traffic, they come up on you in the blink of an eye.

I was still about a mile behind Joe when I noticed he was about to take a wrong turn at the bottom of the exit. I watched helplessly as he turned right instead of left and disappeared. I checked and rechecked our route sheet to see if maybe I was too tired to think clearly and he was correct. But no, the sheet called for a left at the light, just a few miles from our SAG lunch. Joe was definitely heading in the wrong direction.

In the army, soldiers must take an oath when they are sworn in. Written into the creed is the motto "No Man Left Behind." Every now and then, my dad would say this around the house, especially when my brother Matthew and I were younger and our family was getting ready to go on a trip. I usually had my nose in a book and was always the last one to gather my things. Matthew joked that one day everyone would forget about me until halfway to our destination. My father's reply was always, "No man left behind in the Wagner house!" I knew that my dad would never leave anyone behind, and though I wasn't in the mood for any bonus miles in New Mexico, I could never do that, either. Joe was my teammate. I couldn't let him continue to ride in the wrong direction while I headed to lunch, no matter how hungry, dehydrated, and exhausted I was.

When I saw Joe was too far ahead to hear me calling his name, I put as much force into Shiva's pedals as I could muster and somehow managed to sprint after him. When I finally caught up with him after two miles of breathless shouting, one glance at his face told me he knew what he'd done. "We took a wrong turn, didn't we?" he said.

It was a statement, not a question. I wearily nodded, too out of breath to give him verbal confirmation. "Crap!" he exclaimed. He was still fuming as we backtracked our way to the correct route two to three miles away from the SAG stop. Joe thanked me for retrieving him, explaining he'd seen someone on a bicycle heading in that direction and assumed it was an ABB rider. I told him not to give it a second thought. That day Joe learned he could count on me and we became more than teammates; we became friends.

We were extremely hungry and thirsty by the time we pulled into the SAG stop. During RAP the previous evening, Mike had told us we would have the luxury of eating in a volunteer firehouse. It was a welcome relief to be in air-conditioning rather than under the hot desert sun. Just as I rode up to the firehouse and unclipped my shoes, my father and Philippe got back onto the road. I was so angry with my dad for not sticking around for me on what was turning into my most difficult day of the trip. One minute I was determined to keep going. The next I was thinking that the whole journey was a waste of time and that I had no business being with the group. Not having my dad's support was disheartening because if I had ever needed his upbeat attitude, it was on this day. I numbly watched him leave as I limped to the food table.

Sliding to the ground with a few grunts and moans, I quietly ate my lunch and thought about the morning. It had been so physically demanding that I could barely move. But that wasn't all that was worrying me. I felt drained of any kind of motivational emotion. I was a tired sack sagging against the firehouse wall, legs spread out in a quivering heap in front of me. *Who in the world do I think I'm fooling?* I thought. *More important, with whom can I speak about ending this insanity?* But somehow after lunch I got up, filled my water bottles, and together with Joe saddled up to continue our endless trek through the desert of New Mexico.

About an hour after leaving the SAG stop, we ended up on a narrow, paved jogging path that led us past several small neighborhoods filled with pueblo-like houses. Each community made me think I'd been stranded on the desert planet of Tatooine from the original *Star Wars* trilogy. If I hadn't been so mentally drained, I could easily have pictured little Jawas running around or Luke Skywalker's famous Landspeeder trying to outrun the evil Galactic Empire forces.

Pedaling into one of the neighborhoods, I noticed up ahead in the distance that a US Postal Service truck was parked on the side of the road. The traditional square white truck with red-and-blue lettering reminded me of the one that made its rounds through the quiet neighborhoods back home in New Jersey. As we approached, I smelled the exhaust and saw from the blinking hazard lights that the engine was still running. The letter carrier was nowhere to be seen, and the street was deserted.

All at once, I fantasized about throwing Shiva into the nearest brush pile and hijacking the mail truck. I'd drive all the way to Mexico and live out the rest of my days in disgraced exile. I started to plan the details of my escape and tried to figure out how to get enough cash to pay my way down to the border without anyone noticing me. What was the punishment for stealing a government vehicle? Should I throw the mail out of the back of the truck or take it with me? Was the offense worse if I stole the mail too? I wondered how many hours I had before anyone realized I was missing. I didn't consider how ridiculous I'd look driving a mail truck wearing my ABB bicycle gear. I didn't even have real shoes!

With a sinking feeling, I silently passed the truck, alarmed at the fact that I was seriously considering quitting the ride. Of course I wouldn't steal a mail truck, but I began to rehearse what I'd say to my father when I saw him at the end of the day. I'd thank him for thinking of me and tell him the ride had been a nice idea, but it wasn't for me. I'd apologize for wasting a year of my life as well as a lot of his money and say the trip was getting too hard and there was no way I'd make it to the Atlantic Ocean unless it was on a plane.

But even as I rehearsed my speech, I realized if I gave up and went home, I'd be throwing away a once-in-a-lifetime opportunity. As tempting as it would have been to trade in my two wheels for four wheels and a motor, I would have to keep pushing forward under my own power. I knew from experience that life is about making tough choices, and if I quit now, I'd spend the rest of mine regretting the decision. If Joe hadn't been there to keep me company that day, my choice would have been much, much harder. Looking back, I realize we had a major impact on each other, although neither of us said as much. Sometimes it's enough just to be there for someone. You quietly make your presence known, you lead by example, and you give someone the strength to keep going.

The desert roads seemed to stretch forever. As the sun slowly sank into the horizon, deep shadows appeared amid the boulders and the cacti, and my own shadow lengthened across the sand. By the time Joe and I made it to the motel after eleven-and-a-half hours on the road, I was utterly spent. Wheeling Shiva through the sliding glass doors into the lobby, I saw my dad coming down the stairs from the second floor to check on me. The angry feelings from the day faded away as soon as I saw him, and I gave him a weak smile. "Another one in the books, buddy. I'm proud of you for sticking it out!" he said. His words lifted me up for a brief moment until he added, "Oh yeah, there's no elevator in this motel, so you'll have to take the stairs." My smile faltered at the thought of carrying Shiva up flights of stairs. "And one more thing," he said. "There's no hot water." My smile vanished completely. *You've got to be kidding me!*

Carrying Shiva in my shaking arms, I followed my father up two flights of stairs. Normally, I could almost lift her with two fingers, but after such a grueling day on the road, she felt like a sack of rocks. We reached the top of the staircase, and I let her slip through my fingers onto the carpeted hallway with a gentle thump. Once in our room, all I could think about was sleeping in a clean bed. My nightly blog post would have to wait until the next day.

After a quick dinner and an even quicker cold shower, I slid between the sheets and looked over at my father as he slept deeply in his bed. I'd been angry with him for leaving me behind earlier in the day, but I realized that while he tried to be there for me as much as he could while I was growing up, he knew the time was close when he would no longer be able to help me fight my battles. Maybe he knew I needed to get through that day without him and figure it out on my own. I was still grateful to Joe for sticking by my side, but when all was said and done, it had been my feet turning those pedals and my determination that had pushed me forward. Maybe that was the lesson my father needed to teach me—how to deal with extreme discomfort and to feel complete satisfaction knowing I had accomplished exactly what I had set out to do.

Sleep started to overtake me, but I had a smile on my face thinking about my crazy hijacking scheme with me on the lam, hiding out from the authorities as I headed for the Mexican border in a United States mail truck.

Pedal to the Metal

Day 10: Las Vegas, New Mexico-Tucumcari, New Mexico
Distance: 109 Miles
Total: 1,088 Miles

WE LEFT LAS VEGAS UNDER A CLOUDY SKY. DESPITE THE INTENSE soreness in my legs, I was in good spirits. Usually, the ABB team departed each morning in groups of three or four, but that day we bunched together in larger packs of eight or nine as we navigated the streets out of town. Guiding Shiva through the crowd, I was deep in thought when one of the riders behind my dad spoke up. "Hey guys, when was the last time you had the height of your seats measured? You both look a little low in the saddle." It took my brain a few seconds to figure out that the voice belonged to Little Tom. There were two riders in our group named Tom, and we'd given them the nicknames Big Tom and Little Tom. Big Tom was one of the tallest riders and had a powerful, booming voice. Little Tom, one of the fastest riders, wasn't especially fond of his nickname—he wasn't little by any means—but I still called him that in my head because it helped me remember his name.

I looked uncertainly at my dad as he contemplated the question. "We had our seats measured before heading to California," he replied, glancing behind him. I felt Little Tom's eyes focusing on my slowly turning cadence as I eagerly awaited his advice. If he didn't think our seats were high enough, I was more than willing to listen since he was easily one of the most experienced riders on the trip. Any advantage on the road, no matter how small, could mean the difference between an easy or difficult day. "You might want to think about readjusting your seats," Little Tom said. "Nothing crazy, maybe two to three centimeters." His voice grew closer as he pulled up alongside us. "Do it gradually over the course of a few days. Just a few millimeters at a time can make all the difference. Any more can throw you out of whack."

We followed his advice, and with each slight adjustment, I noticed a significant improvement in my cadence and in the smoothness of my ride. Before his suggestion, neither of us was getting the proper extension in our legs. Once we achieved the right seat height, we were obviously generating much more power. I was grateful he had taken an interest in us and had voiced his concern.

My father and I had recently received another great piece of advice, this time from Big Tom about nutritional energy. Ingesting the proper amount of energy on the ride was always a challenge, and a large shipment of something called Honey Stingers caught our eye in Albuquerque. Big Tom graciously agreed to sell us a few and what a difference they made! From that day on, my father and I made sure to include them in our energy stash every morning. It was becoming increasingly clear that even though the team members had started out as strangers in Costa Mesa, we were all in this together.

The morning wore on as we rode through New Mexico's rolling pastures past ranches enclosed in barbed-wire fences. Dozens of mustangs ran in herds of four or five. The steady drum of their hooves beat against the desert soil, and their manes rippled and flowed like silken banners. As the horses galloped past us, we were close enough to see their muscles flex. I admired their fierce strength and the sheer force of their presence amid the emptiness of the landscape. I pictured a race between a stallion running at full speed and me pedaling Shiva as fast as I could. I was pretty sure who would win. If I had only a fraction of the strength in their legs, I could have ridden Shiva all the way to the Atlantic Ocean and back with plenty of energy to spare.

Surprisingly, I was feeling fairly confident. A day earlier, I'd been convinced that the ride was a mistake and that all my training the past year had been a waste of everyone's time. But I hadn't stopped. I'd kept going and, with Joe's support, eventually pedaled into the dark parking lot of the Las Vegas motel. It didn't matter that I'd concocted a half-baked surrender speech for my father or that I'd seriously contemplated stealing a mail truck. What did matter is that every negative, self-critical thought that had entered my brain had been identified and ultimately ignored. I'd heard the familiar negative voices, but with my dream hanging precariously in the balance, I'd pushed myself harder and farther than on any day in my life. Whatever was waiting for me on this ride couldn't possibly be more difficult. (I must add here that ignorance truly is bliss. I hadn't seen anything yet.)

The trip to Tucumcari was shorter than the previous day's 130-plus miles, though at 109 miles, it was just three short of an Iron Man distance. Not long ago the mere thought of riding one hundred miles had been daunting. Now I was well on my way to traveling more than 3,400 miles by the end of the month. Shiva and I had been through a lot, but for the moment I simply enjoyed time in the saddle on flat terrain with a relatively pain-free lower body. Since leaving California, I'd been constantly dealing with some kind of bodily discomfort and had grown attuned to every sensation in my body. Unless there was a new or sharp pain, my mind tuned out the constant muscle aches as if they were background noise or static on an old television. That day, though, even my usual ailments had subsided to a barely noticeable throb.

Pride in what my father and I had achieved up to that point, combined with the mesmerizing sounds of freely running horses, filled me with a quiet sense of wonder and gratitude. By late morning, several riders decided to pick up the pace and sprint ahead, but the rest of us were happy to meander through the rolling hills and the scenic flatlands.

I rode behind Mark, a gentle, kindhearted fellow from California whose claim to fame was that he owned one of the oldest bikes in the group. In fact, it was one of the oldest bikes I'd ever seen, and we joked with him that it belonged in a museum. It was such a relic that its gearshift was on the steel frame, not on the handlebars. Whenever Mark wanted to increase or decrease the resistance of his bike, he had to reach down between his legs and flip the switch located on the middle bar that connected the bike's neck to its handlebars. And did I mention that it was made of steel? I couldn't even guess how much it weighed, but Mark loved his bike and couldn't imagine riding anything else. That was all that mattered.

The desert heat loosened my muscles, and the constant soreness in my legs and my lower back almost vanished. Once again, I marveled at how my body adjusted to the stress of riding. The night before, I could barely bend my legs to pull off my cycling shorts, but less than twelve hours later, I was pedaling relatively pain-free and enjoying the views. Thirty-three miles from the motel, at the top of the Las Vegas Plateau, my father and I saw one of the most astonishing vistas we'd encountered since Sedona. All around us, the towering valley walls stood against the flat expanse of the harsh desert laid out like a tan carpet. I let out an excited yelp that was quickly lost in the rush of the wind as we began our speedy descent toward the valley floor. The only sound I could hear was the steady whirring of Shiva's wheels cutting through the air in front of me.

Rolling faster and faster, we sped down the canyon. It was difficult to concentrate on the road because I kept trying to take in the magnificent sights before me. One of the reasons I'd signed on for this trip was to see America in all her glory. The sheer size and scope of the spectacle before me was overwhelming, and I was reminded of the song "America the Beautiful." I was truly learning firsthand the meaning of the last line, "from sea to shining sea."

We seemed to descend forever. By the time we reached the desert floor, the temperature had once again risen significantly. I took a few gulps of water and rode alongside my dad as the lonely two-lane highway evened out into level terrain again. Up ahead, I saw another cyclist riding solo and enjoying the spectacular views. As we overtook the rider on the left side of the road, Barbara's smiling face surprised us. We called out our greetings and she beamed back at us. "Not far now until the first SAG stop!" she exclaimed. "There's a special surprise waiting for you there!" When we arrived a few miles later, I scanned the dusty lot where the vans were set up and saw our surprise. Someone had written a message on a small whiteboard with a black dry-erase marker: "1,000 Miles in 8 ½ Days!" Pride stirred in my chest. Most of the other riders were long gone, but my dad asked someone to take a photo of us holding the sign before we returned to our bikes.

Back on the road, my thoughts turned to my father's birthday a few days away on May 3. I wanted to make sure we celebrated it as best we could, so a few days earlier I'd secretly asked Barbara if she would buy an ice cream cake and a birthday card. She'd quietly told me at the morning SAG stop that the card was ready for signing and that she would purchase the cake on his birthday. I had to figure out how to get ahead of my dad long enough to tell everyone in the group about my plans.

The flat terrain and my fresh legs presented a perfect opportunity to break away for my secret birthday plan. If I reached our SAG lunch early enough, I could talk to the other riders about the cake and about signing the card. I turned around and told my dad I was going ahead to stretch my legs and then I took off like a shot. The desert sands became a blur of boulders and cacti as I left him behind. Speeding through the desert valley, I realized how much easier I was breathing. I pedaled faster and faster, increasing Shiva's gears until I was at her maximum resistance. What a feeling!

My elation continued until I abruptly reached what the ABB team referred to simply as "the wall." Before we'd started out that morning, Mike had told us about a stretch of road on our route—a 0.7-mile hill with a climb so steep that it almost defied the laws of nature. It reared up suddenly out of the flat expanse of the desert, and I dropped gears so frantically I was sure I'd jam the chain. *I'll need suction cups to keep from tipping over*, I thought.

There is a way to calculate the exact slope of a hill based on a mathematical formula. You divide the height of the hill you're climbing by the length of the climb and multiply that number by a hundred. For instance, a thousand-foot climb over the course of one mile, or 5,280 feet, equals 0.19. That number, multiplied by a hundred, gives you a total graded slope of 19 percent, a relatively easy climb. This beast of a hill, however, was graded past the 60 percent marker. At the time, I wasn't much interested in math calculations, because my legs were screaming in protest and my pedals were barely turning. I grunted, strained, and willed Shiva up that killer hill. My chin was almost on my chest as I stubbornly kept her pedals turning a few inches at a time. My eyes were so focused on the asphalt beneath me that I almost didn't see the brightly colored message sprayed across the road: "Keep Going!"

Despite the difficulty, I smiled and continued inching my way up the slope. Ahead was only more of the relentless hill, but I saw other messages written all the way up to the top. The further I climbed, the more encouraging they became.

"You can do it!"

"Don't stop now!"

"You're almost there!"

Sweat poured off of my forehead. So much for my kick-ass "pedal to the metal" pace just a few minutes earlier. Inch by inch, I pushed and pulled Shiva's pedals until finally I reached the summit. I had conquered "the wall"! I risked one glance down before riding away. The slope looked as steep from the top as it had from the bottom. Still panting, I pushed forward, hoping to find our SAG stop, because I still needed to let everyone know about the plan for my father's birthday.

The stop was only a few minutes farther down the road, and when I pulled in, I was happy to see almost all the other riders were still there. Many were lounging beneath the shade of the single hardy tree dominating the site. Their bikes were spread out between the folding and camping chairs that had been set up with the help of the Four Horsemen, our nickname for the four fastest riders in our group—David of Minnesota, Little Tom of California, Roger of Colorado, and Floris of Amsterdam. The nickname harkened back to the Four Horsemen of the Apocalypse, and it seemed appropriate for these mythical riders able to crush long distances in record time. The Four Horsemen often arrived before or right after the support van pulled into the SAG stop, and they helped the ABB staff set up the site. I didn't learn about their helpful attitudes until halfway through the ride, because my father and I always arrived well past their departure.

I couldn't believe my luck because even the Four Horsemen had stuck around that afternoon, content to enjoy the shade of the tree. I hastily dismounted and began sharing my plan with everyone. I told them Barbara would leave my father's birthday card next to the water station for the next few days so that everyone could sign it in secret. All the riders happily agreed to sign the card as discreetly as possible.

The atmosphere at the SAG lunch was light and playful. Mike even got out a set of golf clubs and hit a few balls out into the desert. When my dad showed up for lunch, I had settled into one of the open chairs and had noticed a delicious addition to the usual assortment of sandwiches, fruits, nuts, and granola bars. Floris explained that back in Holland everyone was celebrating Queen's Day, a national holiday to commemorate the birthday of the former Dutch queen. To celebrate, he had purchased several boxes of pastries for everyone to enjoy. "When you're in a foreign country, you realize how much your country's traditions and holidays mean to you," he said. This made me realize how far some of my teammates were from their homes.

When we finished with lunch and the pastries were gone, my dad and I saddled up and began the last leg of the day's ride. We made it to the motel in great time after only eight hours on the road. It was wonderful to see bright sunshine instead of dark evening shadows as we pulled into the parking lot. After dinner and a stretching session, we headed to RAP. Mike said he hoped we'd enjoyed the beautiful weather that afternoon, because Mother Nature wouldn't be nearly as accommodating over the next few days. A severe storm was approaching with sustained headwinds of 20 mph and gusts from

30 to 40 mph. I noticed that the temperature had already started to drop toward the end of the day. It was only a ninety-seven-mile ride from Tucumcari, New Mexico, to our next town of Dalhart, Texas, but from the grim look on Mike's face, it looked as if we were going to fight for every mile.

Dalhart

Day 11: Tucumcari, New Mexico-Dalhart, Texas
Distance: 97 Miles
Total Distance: 1,185 Miles

THE WIND WHISTLED STEADILY PAST THE MOTEL WINDOW, WAKING ME from a sound sleep. I was struck by how persistent and fierce it sounded as I burrowed deeper under the covers for added warmth. I peered out at my father to see if the noise had wakened him, but he remained fast asleep. I did my usual inventory of sore and tight muscles and discovered I felt pretty good. But then the day's forecast crashed through my consciousness. A nasty storm raged across the Texas flatlands, bringing all kinds of strange weather unheard of this time of year in the Lone Star State. As the storm grew closer to us, temperatures would drop dangerously and snow showers would develop along its path.

Snow. In spring. In Texas. So much for tailwinds gently helping us along in the fourth state of the ride. I threw off the blankets, wincing as my feet contacted an icy cold floor. As I spread my usual assortment of cycling gear onto the bed, I nervously wondered what it would take to survive this day. I rummaged through my luggage in search of my Under Armour thermal shirts and leggings. As I tugged the tight-fitting garments onto my arms, my father sat up in bed, blinking several times in my direction and staring at my attire.

"Think we'll need the jackets?" I joked, holding up our

windbreakers, which up until then had remained packed away. The levity was an attempt to fend off my foreboding thoughts. The whole time I'd been gathering my supplies, the wind continued to howl like an injured animal, and the sound unnerved me. The previous night's message from Mike quickly sank into my father's sleepy brain as well. "Yeah," he said, getting out of bed and reaching for his own thermal gear. "We're going to need them."

He said this without a nervous laugh or a hint of a smile, and this worried me more than the wind. My father always sees the best in any person or situation. The ABB staff and riders found him to be one of the most optimistic people they'd ever met. One day Norman, who joined us after the first week of the ride, told the team in his chirpy Australian accent that if someone hit my father over the head with a hammer, he would simply say, "Good shot, mate!" Today, though, I could tell he was concerned, and I promised myself that whatever happened on the road, I would try my absolute best.

We finished dressing and left for breakfast. The second we stepped out of the motel door, icy wind gusts slammed us back toward the room. My teeth chattered as we proceeded along the walkway. The warmth of the dining room was welcoming, but my stomach felt unsettled and it was difficult to concentrate on eating. Between small bites of powdered eggs and instant oatmeal, I kept looking furtively out of the window. Steely gray clouds blocked any sunlight trying to peek through the darkness. The room was quiet in stark contrast with the usual early morning banter between riders. We all exchanged silent glances as we watched the television in the corner of the room. A worried-looking weatherman pointed vigorously to red-and-yellow cells on a map. The volume was muted, but we knew from his insistent gestures toward the swirling arrows, denoting strong wind currents, that the forecast didn't look good.

My thoughts turned to the night before when Mike gathered us together. "I'm not going to lie to you," he said. "Tomorrow is going to be pretty rough. If at any time you feel uncomfortable, use the signal of tapping the top of your helmet and we'll pick you up right away. Safety is more important than anything else."

There was a bit of light in the sky as we saddled up, so at least it no longer felt like nighttime. But as soon as we left the shelter of the buildings in the town and rolled onto Highway 54, the wind showed its full strength. Grateful for my layer upon layer of cold-weather gear, I didn't feel the wind's bite on any part of my body except for the exposed parts of my face. On the one hand, it would have been helpful to have sunglasses, because each fresh gust brought stinging tears to my eyes. On the other, the glasses would have made it even more difficult to see on such a dark morning.

Trying to keep Shiva as straight as possible, I tucked my head into my shoulders and focused on the wheel turning in front of me. I vaguely knew it wasn't my father's, because he had fallen into the pace line somewhere behind me. For the life of me, though, I couldn't tell who was riding out front. I remember only the endless howling of the wind as we plodded along a shoulder of road barely wide enough to accommodate us. I'd seen sidewalks with more room, and to complicate matters even more, we had to avoid a rumble strip smack in the middle of the shoulder. On that day of all days, I desperately wished we were riding on a quiet country road. To the right was a steep drop into the brush-filled desert. To the left was an uncomfortably close lane of traffic, blowing by us at 75 mph. Each passing vehicle kicked up swirling clouds of dust and sand that were quickly caught up by the relentless wind and thrown into our faces.

It was impossible to hear. Huge trucks seemed to suddenly appear with no distant booming diesel engine or faraway hiss of eighteen wheels. I grew concerned when I remembered Big Dan's advice during our first pace line together near Sedona: "Talking is extremely important when you're moving in a pace line. You always need to let the guys in the front and the guys in the back know what's going on. When you're coming to a stop, when you're about to make a move to the front, or when you spot debris, you need to communicate. It's the best way to stay safe on the road."

On this day there was no way that kind of communication was possible. As soon as any words left my mouth, the roar of the wind and the traffic drowned them out. The only thing I heard was the pounding in my head as I painfully forced each foot down on Shiva's pedals. We were riding at a virtual crawl, and I was glad I hadn't brought my Garmin that day so at least I wouldn't be constantly reminded of our incredibly slow pace.

I picked up my head to try to get my bearings. We were supposed to reach our first SAG stop before the thirty-mile mark, and I desperately wanted to see some sign of our progress. I glanced around and saw that everything basically looked the same as it had when we left earlier that morning—endless stretches of darkened New Mexico landscape broken up by an occasional building or grove of trees. Just before I put my head back down, I saw the familiar shape of one of the ABB support vans out of the corner of my eye. My heart leapt and I hoped that meant the SAG stop wasn't too far ahead.

I was busy wondering who might be sitting in the driver's seat when suddenly the lead pace rider of our group slowed down significantly. I'd taken my eyes off of the rear wheel in front of me for a split second, but that's all it takes for a mistake to happen on the road. By the time I realized the other riders were dropping their speed, I was gaining on the rider in front of me and had just enough time to squeeze my brakes before our bikes collided. I narrowly missed him but another accident was waiting to happen. I'd yelled out in surprise and warning as I was slowing down, but my shout was carried away by the wind. I might as well have said nothing for all the warning the rider behind me got. And that rider was my father.

I felt a sharp push into Shiva's back tire as his bike collided with mine. I wobbled violently. Pulling hard to the left, I barely managed to keep Shiva from careening down the steep desert slope. My father was not as lucky. I watched helplessly as he hit that same drop-off toward the brush and the sand on the right side. Miraculously, he managed to keep his balance and to stay upright as he bounced along the uneven terrain. I watched in horror as he overcorrected his course and cut sharply to the left. With a forceful pull, he tried to wrestle his way back to the middle, but he couldn't stop. For what seemed like an eternity, he bounded into the middle of the highway, completely exposed to traffic. If any vehicles had been on the road during those horrible few seconds, nothing could have prevented him from being hit.

My father finally made it safely back onto the shoulder, but even as he regained his balance and rejoined the pace line, my body was shaking so hard I could barely pedal. The whole incident had happened in less than thirty seconds, but in that half a minute my actions could have cost my father his life. I was trying so hard to be a proper cyclist, paying such close attention to all of the advice our ride leader and other experienced riders had given me. I'd just started to feel comfortable on the road with all the other guys. Yet I'd almost been the cause of a potentially life-threatening accident, with my own father no less. I couldn't even turn around to apologize to him, because I couldn't take my eyes off of the wheel in front of me, and even if I shouted out the words, the wind would swallow them. Knowing my father, he'd probably tell me it was no big deal. He'd say that accidents happen and that I should be more careful in the future. But this was a huge deal to me, and the fact that Mike saw the whole thing from the support van made it even worse.

The image of my father riding helplessly on the highway kept replaying in my mind until I couldn't stand it another minute. "Screw this," I growled under my breath. I needed to be far away, alone with my darkening thoughts and not responsible for anyone else's safety. I checked the highway behind me, saw it was clear, and inched my way onto the road. I immediately met the full assault of the headwinds, but after dropping Shiva's gears one more time, I sped past the rest of the riders. Jan, Max, and Joe couldn't even look up because they were straining so hard against the wind.

In minutes, I was alone with just the endless fury of Mother Nature for company, and boy was she doing her best to blow me over. At least in the pace line there had been a few riders buffering the wind. The going had been slow, but it had been bearable. Riding alone under the full pressure of constant 30 mph winds, I was suddenly unsure of my decision to go solo. But my father's close call streaked across my mind again, and I knew at that moment that I had made a choice. This would be my day—just me and the weights around my neck that I'd been carrying for so long. I had no idea how it would turn out, but I knew the time had come to face my demons head-on.

I reached the first SAG stop, and other than apologizing to my father and letting my teammates know I'd be riding without them, I stayed distant and silent. Jan sensed something was wrong but said only, "You gotta ride your own way, Eric. Do what you need to do," as he patted my shoulder. I looked at him and nodded in reply, still saying nothing. Instead, I loaded up my pockets with as much food as they would hold, because I had no idea how long it would take me to get to the SAG lunch or if I would even make it there. Judging by how long it had taken me to get to the first stop, this would be a long day.

Pedaling back onto the road, I started feeling calmer, almost soothed by my solitude. But as the miles wore on, the wind's roars turned into shrieks as the temperature continued to drop with startling speed. Despite my many layers of gear, a numbing cold worked its way through my leggings and the insulated booties encasing my feet until I had no sensation in my lower body. The only way I could tell I was moving forward was by watching Shiva's wheels turn ever so slowly. I dropped her gears again and again as I plodded through the harsh elements.

The fierce wind cried relentlessly in my ears until I began to hear an equally fierce noise. I didn't recognize it at first but soon realized it was my own anguished voice. Again and again, I let out screams that were immediately stolen by the storm. All my feelings of anger, sadness, doubt, and confusion boiled dangerously close to the surface, and with a howl from somewhere deep inside me that I didn't know existed, I felt a crack in my mental dam. Everything I'd been holding inside—questions without answers, uncertainty about my life, the feeling I'd disappointed the people who loved me, the guilt over my actions in college—worked its way out of the dark space of my heart.

I'd spent almost a year of my life digging a gigantic hole, and even though I'd done everything I could to climb out—graduating from the college I loved, trying to get back into good physical shape, and apologizing over and over to my family and friends—a part of me had never left that hole. It was a place of quiet desperation and fear where, despite all my best efforts, I still felt my life slipping through clenched fists.

Then questions started rising up inside of me, roaring more loudly than the wind.

Who was I? Was I White Hat Eric? Was I Black Hat Eric? Did it even matter?

A familiar pain clutched my chest—the same pain I felt that fateful morning in March 2011 when I looked down the path of my life with awful clarity. I recalled the helpless look I'd seen in the mirror every morning as I numbly brushed my teeth. I would ask my reflection, *Who are you and where's Eric?* After a while, I was careful not to look anymore, because I didn't recognize the person staring back at me.

The questions arose with alarming speed and intensity. They grew until they pressed against the back of my teeth before bursting forth as something more raw and primal than the storm. I screamed into the wind, "Who am I? Who am I? Who am I?"

Again and again the words were lost, but then … something happened. I sensed a slight release; the pain in my heart eased a fraction, and the chains around my neck felt a tiny bit looser. I let out more and more angry screams, each rising and falling on the wind as if I were trying to match Mother Nature's ferocity or, better yet, beat her at her own game. Each fault, embarrassment, and feeling of uncertainty that I'd allowed to consume me forced its way out of my chest. The wind nearly knocked me off Shiva as I wailed.

And with the next gust, answers began arriving.

"I am Eric Wagner! I am a JMU Duke! I am a writer!" Before I knew what was happening, I was yelling my school chant—"JMU Dukes, Dukes, Dukes!"

Each chant brought me renewed strength as I continued against the fury of the storm. I shouted out the names of all the people who cared about me and loved me unconditionally. My friends and their families from Sandshore Elementary School, Mount Olive Middle School, and Mount Olive High School, who had been in my life for so long I couldn't remember a time without them. My friends and professors from James Madison University, who did everything they could to support me when I finally admitted I needed help. My brother Matthew, whom I looked up to so much because he lived life on his own terms and always believed in following his passions. My mother, Lisa, who immediately dropped everything and drove to my side when I told her I was in trouble. And my father, Ralph. He was out there somewhere in the same horrible storm. This journey certainly hadn't been easy for him either, but he'd never complained when he was sick, never stopped supporting or encouraging me, and above all, never stopped pedaling.

Letting go of months and years of sadness and regret was the first step toward finding my old self. If I looked into the mirror at that moment, would I see glimpses of Eric again? For the first time I started to believe that I might. My eyes stung and not just from the swirling dirt and grit. The dam was breaking and I could no longer hold anything back. Tears rolled down my face before being dried almost instantly by the wind. It didn't matter because no one was there to see or hear me.

Through blurry vision, I spotted the second group of riders a few miles later. They were riding in a close-knit, single-file line along the shoulder of the highway. I saw a helmet turn in my direction as I silently rode past them. I didn't know it at the time, but that was the only day I'd be the fifth rider in line. Aside from the Four Horsemen, nobody on the road was ahead of me. At that point, though, I was far from caring. All I knew was that the overwhelming emotions pent up inside of me were doing everything they could to break free and that they were finally winning. With each passing mile in Texas, the fire inside me slowly burned itself out.

Riding into the SAG lunch, I could barely move my cold and weary legs. I gently placed Shiva against a wooden post holding up a sad-looking picnic table and noticed that aside from Mike and Barbara, I was alone. During the last hour, I'd seen the ABB support vans passing by with several bikes attached to the roof, my father's included. At the time I had been too consumed in my own thoughts to wonder what had happened. As I sat on the bench with a small plate of food on top of my trembling legs, I asked Mike where everyone was, and he said that many riders had opted to be picked up in the van and brought to the motel. I nodded and stiffly returned to my lunch as a few riders limped in from the cold. Soon we were all huddled together next to the shelter of the support van.

When it came time to saddle up and ride the last twenty miles to the motel, I looked at my shivering body and out at the road. In the short time we'd been eating, the weather had grown even more hostile. I thought about all that had happened to me since I had started out earlier that morning. I knew I was no longer the same young man, hell-bent to ride every single mile to prove to myself and to everybody else that I was becoming a better person. I knew it was okay to ask for help and that this didn't mean I was a failure. That day, for the first time in a long time, I started to forgive myself.

I told Mike that I also was done for the day, and he accepted my decision without comment. He'd noticed my mistake in the pace line, and I knew it would be only a matter of time before it was addressed. Still, I was certain I'd be able to handle whatever Mike needed to teach me without immediately thinking I was not fit for the trip. I'd made a mistake, but I had learned from it and I'd do my best to never let it happen again.

I helped Mike load Shiva onto the rack atop the van and gratefully settled into its warm interior. I wasn't the only one who realized conditions had turned from challenging to dangerous. Mark and George shared the ride to the motel with me, and we took turns declaring how difficult the day had been. I told the two of them that at one point while I was still riding Jody had sped by me exclaiming, "Can you believe we're paying to do this?" We passed a few hardy souls who refused to come in from the storm, but I knew the decision was a personal one for each rider. I'd done what I felt was best for me without guilt.

That night at RAP, we gathered in the motel's conference room and went over the ride. I appreciated that Mike didn't single out my mistake. Instead, he reminded all of us to always be aware of our surroundings and to be vigilant on the road. "It takes only one mistake to end your or a teammate's journey," he said, glancing for a brief second in my direction.

It's said that in times of great hardship, men band together. I felt exactly that as I looked around at my ABB team. During the next few weeks, whenever the road became long and difficult, we'd look at each other and simply say, "Dalhart." For my teammates that word meant they could surely handle anything else thrown at them on the road. For me, it meant my life was finally headed on the right course.

Our Achilles' Heel

Day 12: Dalhart, Texas-Liberal, Kansas
Distance: 113 Miles
Total Distance: 1,298 Miles

WAKING UP FROM ONE OF THE DEEPEST SLEEPS OF MY LIFE, I TRIED TO open my eyes and gasped. For one horrifying moment, I couldn't see a thing! Panic gripped me until a tiny sliver of light appeared in front of my face and the world revealed itself in blurry detail. I heaved a sigh of relief. I wasn't blind! The swirling dust and sand on the road had made its way out of my eyes during the night, and my eyelids were stuck together. I gently coaxed my gummed lids further apart until the blurriness faded.

Mike had informed us at RAP the night before that he was canceling our 113-mile bike ride to Liberal, Kansas. He'd done such a thing only three times in his career, he explained, adding that the ride from Tucumcari to Dalhart had been one of the worst he had ever experienced. Nobody was surprised that he had canceled the ride, because we knew how Mike felt about safety and about keeping his riders out of harm's way. We'd all reach our next town by van instead of by bicycle.

As soon as we learned we'd have an unscheduled day off, Jan decided to pick up a twelve-pack, and he invited us all to join him. When I walked into his room, the heater was blowing on high, providing welcome warmth against the raging elements just past the window. We had been out of the storm for forty-five minutes, and I was finally beginning to feel my fingers and my toes. I tossed back a cold one as we talked about college and how his children were still finding their paths in life.

"My daughter graduated a few years ago," Jan said after a sip. "My son goes to Virginia Tech, and he's been traveling abroad for the past several weeks." We talked for a few more minutes, and after we finished our cans, I thanked Jan for the beer and the conversation. It had been nice to talk about something other than how sore we were or about how grueling the past few days had been. As I was leaving, he gave me a few extra cans to share with whoever else might enjoy one.

When I got to my room, I handed beers to my dad and to Joe as they settled into chairs and searched for an NBA playoff game on television. They couldn't find it on any of the channels, so I volunteered to ask the clerk at the front desk. The lobby was in a separate building, and as soon as I opened the door, the fury of Snowstorm Achilles was once again upon me. A snowstorm doesn't normally warrant a name, but due to its unseasonable appearance on the Midwest plains, meteorologists had made an exception.

I wholeheartedly agreed with them, especially when I learned that during our ride to Dalhart, the wind gusts had reached an impressive 40 mph, with windchills lowering the real-feel temperature to nineteen degrees. Three days earlier I had been battling ninety-four-degree heat. It's safe to assume I'll never see a seventy-five-degree temperature difference in such a short time again. And I'm sure I never want to!

I closed the door and bent low against the onslaught of the wind. The friendly clerk had the game on in the lobby and told me the correct channel. When I returned to the room slightly frosted, we switched to the Boston Celtics game. Suddenly the air was filled with the sound of beer cans popping open as we toasted our upcoming day off. Although we did nothing more than sit comfortably in our motel room watching the basketball game, it meant a great deal to me. We had endured the worst conditions this ride had to offer and had survived. Somehow watching the game seemed like a rite of passage. We weren't drinking any special kind of brew, but I remember the cool texture of the aluminum can in my hands and the sense of contentment that spread through my body while I sipped.

My dad had been raised on the Boston Red Sox side of Connecticut, and Joe was from New England, so the two of them shared a love for the Boston Celtics. I didn't particularly care which team won, but it was fun to listen to them groan with each error the Celtics made and to hear them cheer after a good play on offense. That night I went to bed with a feeling of camaraderie. I was one of the guys.

The next morning there was no urgency to return to the road. Once I washed out my sore eyes, I packed up my contact lenses and put on what my father calls my black Clark Kent eyeglasses. At breakfast I saw I wasn't the only one with battle scars from the storm. Eric from Pennsylvania was wearing an eye patch because one of his corneas had dried out in the relentless wind.

We stepped onto the sidewalk with our luggage in tow and again were assaulted by freezing winds. It was a bustling scene of ordered chaos as bundled-up cyclists ferried their luggage from the parking lot to the blue ABB trailer. I hadn't seen any snowfall, but I could feel the storm's anger as each forceful gust threatened to send us sprawling onto the hard ground. I quickly passed my bags into Jim's waiting hands and gritted my teeth against the icy cold cutting into the exposed skin between my gloved hands and the sleeves of my windbreaker.

Because there were only two ABB vans and more than twenty cyclists, Mike divided us into two trips. My dad and I were in the first group to leave, but we were placed in different vans. Mike was standing on the roof rack of my assigned van, and after lifting Shiva into his hands I quickly ducked inside and out of the wind. Jody was contentedly sitting by the window, and I squeezed in next to him with a friendly nod. George and several other cyclists filed in after me.

As we drove along the lonely highway, a few of the guys nodded off. I couldn't blame them; there wasn't a lot to see. The skies were the same leaden gray they'd been all of the previous day, and it seemed as if the weather had scared off cars and trucks. Occasionally, the van rocked from side to side in the furious wind. The only break in the monotonous plains was the occasional group of corn silos and eventually a sign informing us that the extensive farmlands of Texas had been replaced by the extensive farmlands of Kansas.

It felt strange to cross state lines in the seat of a van rather than on the saddle of Shiva. As grateful as I was to be warm and dry, I felt the tug of the road. My feelings were short-lived because piles of snow from Achilles soon began appearing against the almost-black Kansas soil. It was bizarre to see snow in the middle of America's heartland, especially in spring. Even George, who had been chatting away since he got into the van, paused his running dialogue about Margaret Thatcher and simply watched the snowdrifts dotting the tilled fields.

Eventually, Jody, who'd been politely listening to our conversation, reached into a travel bag on his lap and pulled out an e-reader. "What are you reading?" I asked as it silently powered up. He handed me the handheld device, and I saw *A Tale of Two Cities* by Charles Dickens appear on the screen. For a while, I had owned an iPad in college and had used it to read books and to take notes in class. When I first received it, the idea of instantly downloading books with the press of a button had seemed new and exciting, but the novelty quickly wore off and I returned to regular printed books. There was something about holding a book and turning pages that I found far more appealing than the instant gratification of an electronic device.

Navigating the table of contents in Jody's e-book with gentle strokes of my fingertips, I felt the same uncomfortable sensation I had sitting in my journalism classes in college. I remembered my professors talking about the shifting nature of journalism and about how the industry was evolving at a faster pace than anyone could have anticipated. Many professors believed that with the rise of online media sources like blogs, Facebook, Google, and Twitter, the traditional role of the journalist was quickly fading. Local newspapers were shrinking at an alarming rate and going out of business every day. Circulation was dwindling as more and more readers turned to online news sources, books, and magazines. Borders, the second-largest bookstore chain in the country, had recently gone out of business, with the last of its stores closing in September 2011.

The device I was holding had been partly, if not mostly, responsible. I handed it back to Jody. "Good book?" I asked. *A Tale of Two Cities* had been on my list of books to read for some time. "I like it," he replied in a slow, thoughtful tone. Jody rarely spoke, and when he did, he chose his words carefully. "The dialogue and the words used are much different than in more modern books." He leaned in and double-tapped the screen, highlighting a word. Instantly, a variety of possible meanings appeared beneath his index finger, including one selection simply labeled "dictionary." "I use this thing all the time," Jody admitted, as if he were embarrassed by the fact that he didn't know exactly how people spoke and wrote more than a hundred years ago. I thanked him for letting me see his e-book and left him to his reading.

I settled back into my seat, thinking about books, reading, and writing, which bring me more joy than almost anything else in life. Books are like oxygen to me. Left to my own devices, I'd read all day long. In grade school, I'd hide a book under my desk just so I could keep reading. My third-grade teacher once told my parents that I was the only student she'd ever had to ask to stop reading. My mother would watch me walk home from the bus stop day after day with my nose inside a book, oblivious to the playful bantering of my friends.

I spent four years in college continually trying to adjust my romantic notion of what I believed journalism to be and to embrace what it had become. I preferred getting ink on my hands from handling a newspaper to searching a computer for information. When I write, I like having smeared ink or graphite on my left hand because it allows more of a connection with the words on the paper. Was there a seat for a traditional, old-school journalist like myself at this modern online table of writers?

These thoughts had been whirling in my head ever since my first journalism professor had explained what was happening in the media world. Instead of excitement at these new opportunities, I had seen the death of my cherished images of sitting in a bustling newsroom with reporters racing to meet a deadline or of walking a beat with a tape recorder in my pocket, a pad of legal paper under my arm, and a pen in my eager hands as I chased after my next story. I had allowed this fear to settle over my dream of being a writer, the only thing I had ever wanted to do. I wasn't just chasing an occupation; I was chasing a dream I'd had since I was old enough to pick up a book.

While my friends all seemed to settle comfortably into their chosen majors of business, history, or finance, I began to feel alienated. There was no way I could separate my passion from my occupation, and if I wasn't a writer, who was I? What about making a difference in the world with my words? The thought of trying to find something else to do with my life paralyzed me with uncertainty and fear. Instead of voicing my concerns, I steadily ignored them. Instead of asking for help, I started to numb myself from my growing anxiety.

The miles passed quickly traveling in the van instead of pedaling on our bikes, and we pulled into the motel parking lot before noon. After I received Shiva from her perch, I met my dad in our room. He told me some of the guys were going out for an early lunch. "I think I'm going to take a nap," he said, "but if you go with them, will you bring me back something?" I nodded and left for the lobby where Joe, Big Tom, Jim J, and Big Dan were waiting. I'd ridden with Joe and Big Dan, but I didn't know Big Tom or Jim very well

A small yellow taxi van pulled up, and we all piled in. The restaurant we picked was mostly empty, but it had an interesting atmosphere. Stop signs had been hung next to team jerseys and other sports memorabilia, and with all its tropical decorations, the bar looked like it belonged at the edge of a beach. When the waitress arrived, a few guys ordered beers while I stuck with water. The days were hard enough for me without risking dehydration.

As we sat around the table, I started learning about my new friends. If you took the character Kramer from the sitcom *Seinfeld*, mellowed him out just a little, and gave him one of the deepest voices possible, you'd have Big Tom. He was six feet with a head full of dark, curly hair. He talked about his daughters and about his time serving as a military pilot in Germany.

Jim, I would soon discover, was one of the toughest, most interesting people on the road. I loved hearing his stories about hiking the Appalachian Trail, his intention to climb Mount Kilimanjaro after he finished our ride, and his days as a cage fighter. "When I was younger, I had a lot of energy, and there wasn't a whole lot to do in my town," Jim explained, "so I would drive about forty minutes away to this seedy bar and fight people." Back then the term "cage fighting" hadn't been coined. He said there were few rules (no eye gouging, fishhooking, or shots to the groin), and the ring was enclosed by a metal fence. All this pointed to one conclusion: men were fighting in a cage! Jim proudly told me that he'd never been knocked down, although in one match he'd been knocked out while on his feet and the referees had been forced to call the fight. I'm still not sure how that happens, but I didn't doubt his word for a second.

As usual, the menu choices for lunch consisted mostly of burgers and sandwiches. I would have loved to order something with a few fresh vegetables, but in this part of the country, carbohydrates and animal protein ruled. I opted for buffalo wings, a hamburger weighing more than a pound, and a huge side order of french fries. I ordered the same meal to go for my dad.

While we waited for our food, Big Tom looked up from his drink and asked in a quiet voice if we had noticed anything unusual about our cab driver. I thought about the young woman behind the wheel. She hadn't said much except that she would pick us up after we were done eating. Now that he mentioned it, though, I had noticed that she wore large sunglasses despite the overcast skies.

When no one answered, Big Tom wondered aloud whether she was a victim of domestic abuse. As he elaborated on the characteristics of an abused woman, it was clear to the rest of us that he was speaking about a topic he knew well. "Is anyone here a writer?" he asked. I raised my hand with a confused look on my face.

"I've been thinking about researching and writing about the negative effects of alcohol on the family unit," he told me.

I was shocked to hear one of my new friends raise such a difficult subject, and I didn't know how to respond. Our lunch arrived, and I gratefully dug into my meal. Another rider told us about a brother who'd been lost to drug addiction, and soon my companions were embroiled in a lengthy discussion of painful experiences involving drugs and alcohol. Remaining silent, I tried to focus on my hamburger as the rest of the group listed family members and friends who'd died from their addictions or might as well have for all the good they now had in their lives.

The more they talked about their experiences, the more I thought about my own relatives and friends. I couldn't bear to imagine people I loved sitting around a table explaining how my actions had hurt them. The more I listened, the more amazed I became at how common my situation had been. Obviously I did not own the rights to confused choices or sad emotions. These men had offered their own stories and, without knowing it, had helped me realize that everyone has an Achilles' heel. But still I stayed silent without joining the discussion. I wasn't ready to share anything about my past, and by the time we'd settled our bills, I was more than happy to leave.

Clutching my dad's doggy bag, I waited with the guys for our cab to arrive. The driver still wore her dark glasses, and I made it a point to smile at her as I climbed into the backseat. I hoped we had been wrong about her situation, but I had a sad feeling that Big Tom was right. It's true you never know the story behind each person.

On the way back to the motel, I stared out of the window at the hostile weather and saw things hadn't improved one bit. The wind was still fierce and the skies still dark with the threat of snow. Once we arrived, I quietly opened the door to our room and tiptoed over to my dad's bed. I deposited his lunch on the end table next to his sleeping form and flopped down onto my own bed. I tried to follow his lead and take a nap but couldn't fall asleep. I felt the road calling me back to my journey to the Atlantic, so I powered up my laptop and counted down the hours until it was time for RAP.

Blood Brothers

Day 13: Liberal, Kansas-Dodge City, Kansas
Distance: 82 Miles
Total Distance: 1,380 Miles

SLUGGISHLY COLLECTING MY SCATTERED GARMENTS, I COULDN'T HELP but feel like I was moving underwater. My stomach gurgled fitfully, and my thoughts felt as slow as my digestive track. I couldn't remember the last time I'd eaten a heavy meal like the one I'd devoured at lunch the previous day. At one point I even tried a questionable lump of a vegetable that Big Dan called okra. I'd never heard of such a plant—nor had I ever experienced something so completely fried in fat. After a few bites I stopped caring about the strangeness of the name and just called it delicious. My dad had awakened from his nap ravenous and had scarfed down every morsel of the lunch I'd brought back from the restaurant. We spent the rest of the day lounging in the motel's hot tub in an effort to keep our muscles loose and surfing through the limited number of cable channels.

When my dad rolled over to say "Good morning," I realized with a jolt that it was May 3—his birthday! After all of my careful planning, I'd finally be able to celebrate his special day. The riders and the ABB staff had signed his birthday card, and Barbara had told me she would pick up the cake during her supply run. I'd even asked Joe if he would feel comfortable saying a few words on my father's behalf, and he had agreed. The three of us were becoming very close and were almost always together, bringing up the rear.

At times it felt odd that I'd known Joe and the rest of the riders for less than a month, because I felt a growing bond with so many of them. Many times I'd come close to throwing in the towel and quitting the ride, but I kept pedaling simply because of the reassuring presence or encouraging word of a fellow rider. I often found comfort just knowing they were on the road with me.

That was especially true of Barry. He had ridden with my father and me on the first day when we'd accidentally gone an extra ten miles after getting lost. He'd ride with us on occasion, but he would also mingle with some of the faster riders or go solo. Whenever Barry rode in the back with us, he brought a sense of quiet energy that would renew my aching muscles. I loved following the stuffed teddy bear that he secured to the back of his bike with a bungee cord. I soon got into the habit of calling the little guy Barry's Bear. It was almost as much a member of the group as anyone else on the ride.

During our initial orientation in California when each rider spoke about his reasons for riding, Barry's story made me listen with wide-eyed disbelief. I knew that he suffered from serious health problems and that he was riding for a charitable cause, but when it was just the two of us riding on a quiet country road on our way to Dodge City, I learned much more about my inspirational team member.

The wind whistled past the empty cornfields and the tractor lots lining the highway and rocked us gently side to side on our bikes. The only break in the scenery was an occasional tractor lumbering by or a pickup truck with a sunburned face peering out of the window. Breaking the silence, I asked Barry whether he had a wife waiting for him back home. I hadn't noticed a wedding band on his hand, and I was fishing for some common-ground topics. I'd asked the question without considering its weight given Barry's diagnosis of both hemophilia and HIV. "No, haven't made that long walk yet," he replied in a lighthearted tone, his eyes fixed on the road ahead as he slowly turned his pedals. Once he answered, I was embarrassed at my lack of consideration.

Even before Barry had been born, fate had dealt him a tough hand. At a young age, he'd been diagnosed with hemophilia, the blood disorder that affects the body's ability to clot properly when there is a wound or internal damage. Growing up, I'd known a boy who had this condition. He always had to be extremely careful when he played with other children and even more careful when he participated in sports. Once during a basketball game, I saw him elbowed in the face during a scuffle for a rebound. Blood streamed onto his jersey at an alarming rate as parents and coaches rushed toward him. Thanks to modern medicine, he'd been okay, but back in the '60s when Barry was born, those lifesaving medications weren't readily available.

As we rode along, Barry explained to me how hemophilia had weakened his joints over time, causing deterioration and inflammation. Even during the toughest climbs of our ride, I noticed he would never get up out of the saddle and put pressure on his weakened knees. To make matters worse, when Barry was in high school he received a blood transfusion tainted with the HIV virus. At the time, HIV was so new and misunderstood that those who contracted it often were met with suspicion or even violence. Barry told me that he knew people with the virus who had lost their jobs, their homes, and even their families. Sadly, his brother had died from complications resulting from the disease and the medications used to treat it.

As I listened in quiet disbelief, Barry recounted how, after a long, painful struggle, he found himself sitting on a cold steel table facing a doctor who gently recommended that he get his affairs in order. Determined to change the course of his life, Barry searched for and discovered a new treatment that miraculously worked. As his health recovered, he began exercising to build up his strength. Because his weakened joints could never tolerate running, he rode a bicycle, eventually deciding he wanted to travel across the United States to raise money to help others diagnosed with hemophilia. He'd been given a second chance at life, he told me, and he wanted to give that same chance to those without access to lifesaving treatments.

"In less fortunate countries," he explained, "people suffering from hemophilia live in fear every day of being injured, because there is no way to stop the bleeding."

Barry trained to ride across the United States for an international nonprofit called Save One Life. When he first outlined his plans to ABB officials, he was met with raised eyebrows and incredulous expressions. Riding across America on a bicycle is difficult enough with the healthiest body in the best of conditions. What if Barry were injured while riding? What if he couldn't keep up with the other riders? Liability and insurance issues had to be considered. But Barry's convincing argument won over the ABB team, and he received permission to ride in 2012.

While I was walking across the stage at James Madison University to receive my college diploma, Barry had already raised more than $35,000 on his first ride. That ride was such a huge success that Barry signed up for the 2013 Fast America Ride with ABB—the much more aggressive thirty-three-day, 3,400-mile journey from Costa Mesa, California, to Amesbury, Massachusetts. Lucky for us, it was the same ride my father and I were on.

We pedaled in silence for a few miles until Barry spoke again to tell me a story. "On my first ride with ABB, I was pedaling my way through North Dakota and came across a sign for this little museum," he said. "It was on the side of the road and featured antique farming tools. I was tired, sore, and wasn't really in the mood to stop, but I did. You couldn't have imagined how surprised I was when I walked in and was greeted by two old folks who had actually lived through the Dust Bowl. They talked to me the whole time I toured their museum, and I hung on every word. They were fascinating people. Who knows if they're still there? The point is, Eric, when this is all over and you get back to the real world, you won't remember the pain in your legs or how tired you were. You'll remember the amazing things you saw and the connections you made when you took that road less traveled. You never know what you'll find off the beaten path."

We fell into a companionable silence for a while. I thought of the small towns and the tiny shops we'd passed since we'd left the Pacific Ocean behind. Each town held a story and each store a secret I'd never know unless I was willing to pursue these things. I vowed to take more time to savor each experience, and I knew I'd never forget Barry's advice.

We reached Dodge City and my thoughts turned to my father's birthday celebration. Just as RAP was ending, I nodded excitedly toward Barbara. With a big smile she brought out his cake while I handed him his birthday card, full of signatures. His smiled widened as he read each message on the card, and I knew he was touched that we had remembered his birthday. "I love it," he said. I beamed with pride. It was the end of a long day, but everyone mustered the energy to make my dad feel special. To this day the card proudly hangs on the wall of his office.

As Barbara cut pieces of birthday cake, Joe stood and addressed everyone because I still wasn't ready to talk in front of a crowd. I didn't want to ruin my dad's big day by saying the wrong thing or becoming flustered. Joe said it was a pleasure getting to know my father and wished him the best on the ride and during the rest of the year. We all sang "Happy Birthday" as Barbara handed out plates of melting ice cream cake. Phil spoke while the slices were passed around.

"Hey guys, I would like to take a moment too and thank Ralph for his generous donation to the Wounded Warrior Project," he said. "His contribution has brought us that much closer to our goal." When I first met Phil, he showed me a video that a few local high school kids had helped him make to raise awareness and contributions for his charity, which offers programs for wounded veterans. Phil and my dad had a lot in common. Both were tough army rangers but also had a huge capacity for love and generosity. Phil was a gung-ho guy who usually could be found riding strong with Jim. I knew he was a great person the first time I met him.

That night, Joe, my dad, and I watched the last Celtics game in the motel bar. I was minding my own business and didn't see the two very tipsy Kansas girls behind me. Before I knew it, one of them walked past me and pinched my rear end. I almost jumped off of my barstool and looked back to see them laughing hysterically. They weren't the only ones laughing. Big Dan had told them I was sad about the basketball game and needed some cheering up. I could hear his booming laughter clear across the bar!

Though I'd laughed good-naturedly at being the target of the joke, I found myself still mulling over my conversation with Barry. For the first time I wasn't thinking about how the ride could teach me lessons that would change my life. I was thinking that it already had.

Let's Talk about Ralph

Day 14: Dodge City, Kansas-Great Bend, Kansas
Distance: 84 Miles
Total Distance: 1,464 Miles

WE LEFT DODGE CITY WITH ONLY EIGHTY-FOUR MILES UNTIL OUR NEXT stop in Great Bend, Kansas. The temperatures were well below freezing with strong 30 mph headwinds that had arrived during the night. There wasn't a cloud in the sky, yet we could hardly feel the sun's rays. To make matters worse, there wasn't a tree or a building around for miles to slow down Mother Nature. I was bundled in my usual cold-weather gear, but nothing seemed to provide much warmth as we traveled across the empty farmlands. On paper, the day's ride was supposed to be an easy one, but I was quickly learning that even the best-laid plans are often just best guesses.

The famous frontier town swiftly disappeared behind us, and there was nothing but the flat pancake terrain of the Wheat State ahead for miles. Thankfully, the route sheet clipped securely to my handlebars was short in its instructions for the day. We slowed our pace to conserve energy, so all I needed to do was lower my head into the teeth of the wind and keep putting one pedal in front of the other. As usual, the other riders faded into the distance ahead of my dad and me.

I was still thinking about my conversation with Barry. After I had heard his story, the obstacles I faced on the road—or in life—didn't seem quite so overwhelming. If anything, the fact that I was riding under an impossibly large Kansas sky with my father by my side, seeing parts of America that many people would never get to experience, made me feel lucky. Even when my legs protested and my lower back complained, I focused on the fact that there were people in the world with struggles far greater than my own.

Each new sunrise brought another chance to look inward and to ask myself the tough questions that in the past had sent me scrambling for quick distractions. So what if I was scared and uncertain about the course of my life? The idea that uncertainty could also be exciting had cautiously entered my thoughts. I'm sure Barry never believed his life would present such intense health challenges, but here he was, riding to help others less fortunate than himself instead of wallowing in his misfortune. And here I was, fortunate enough to be riding with guys from all walks of life showing incredible commitment to seeing the ride through. I was realizing that my bicycle journey was beginning to represent my life—full of twists and turns, some right, some wrong; stretches of calm and peace; moments of doubt, exhilaration, and terror, and all along, the unknown a constant companion.

Despite the wind gusts, I felt stronger than I had in a long time, so I pushed past my father to take the lead, hoping to offer him the opportunity to draft behind me. After a few miles, I looked back to discover he was a few hundred feet behind instead of keeping close to me. His pedals were barely turning in their sprockets, and when I slowed down enough to let him catch up, I felt as if I was hardly moving at all. When he finally reached me, I asked if he was okay. Rather than answer, my dad shook his head and kept riding. With the wind swirling around us, I couldn't tell if he was shaking off the question, denying there was something wrong, or acknowledging he'd heard me. But from the grimace on his face, it looked like he was in a great deal of discomfort.

Finally, he came to a complete stop and got off of his bike. I slowed to a stop a few feet ahead and shuffled backward along the highway. My father quickly waved me away with a frustrated tone in his voice as he shouted above the wind, "It's my back. It just needs to loosen up. I need to stretch for a while, so you keep going. I'll catch up." He placed a gloved hand against his bike to steady himself and bent low to the ground. Watching him continue to stretch, I again marveled at his determination. I wasn't surprised; his fortitude had begun long before we'd ridden our first ABB mile.

My father became very ill three months before we were scheduled to leave for California. He went to the doctor, started on antibiotics, and stopped training for a week to recover. Unfortunately, the medication wasn't strong enough and his symptoms persisted, so the doctor suggested he have a chest X-ray to rule out pneumonia. When the X-rays revealed he didn't have pneumonia, he was sent home. When his condition steadily worsened over the next few days, my mother threw down the gauntlet and brought him back to the doctor's office, saying she wasn't leaving until someone figured out what was wrong. (Note: don't mess with an Italian mom!) Only then did someone realize that while the X-rays confirmed my dad did not have pneumonia, they did show he had a terrible case of bronchitis, which nobody had told the doctor.

Once on the proper antibiotics he slowly improved, but by the time the mistake was discovered, my dad had lost three weeks of training. Because he had lost so much time on the bike, he tried to jump right back into the strict training schedule he had set up for us. Subsequently, he injured his lower back and needed another couple of weeks to heal before he could get back in the saddle.

So less than three months before we were scheduled to ride 3,400 miles across the country in thirty-three days, my father had missed almost six weeks of training. Although I didn't voice my opinion, I worried he wouldn't be able to overcome such difficult setbacks. But I knew that my dad never shied away from a challenge, and that if anyone could do it, he could. He trained as much as possible until our departure, constantly reassuring us he was feeling "on top of his game." I have to admit that more than once my mother and I quietly raised an eyebrow at each other during his enthusiastic declarations.

Now it seemed his back injury had resurfaced on that lonely stretch of Kansas highway. I suspected he'd never gotten over it and had been riding through the pain all along. (I learned after the ride that I was absolutely right.) Seeing I hadn't gone ahead, he again waved me away. "I'll catch up," he said. His grim expression told me otherwise, so I shook my helmeted head and bent down to touch my toes. *I might as well get in a little stretching time, too,* I thought. "What am I going to do?" I said. "Hang out at the motel while you're out here in this?" I gestured at shimmering waves of wheatgrass being flattened by the wind. "C'mon! We're Team Wagner! No soldier left behind!" After a few minutes, we got back in our saddles and set out for the first SAG stop.

We couldn't have gone more than five miles when my dad slowed to a stop again. I looked at my watch. At this rate, it was going to be a very long day. Again and again, he tried to wave me away. Each time, I shrugged and stubbornly stayed by his side. I could tell he was frustrated that his body was struggling. After a few more stretches, we got back in our saddles and kept riding. That became our routine—stopping, stretching, and continuing a few miles at one of the slowest paces I'd ever experienced. At times we were moving so slowly that every muscle in my body was screaming to pick up the pace or risk toppling over. But each time I wanted to get up and sprint, I reminded myself my dad would never leave me behind if the roles were reversed and I was in that condition.

We plodded along as morning turned into afternoon. *Just a little bit farther,* I thought, silently willing my father along each time we got back in our saddles. We made our way through small Kansas town after small Kansas town until finally we stopped for our SAG lunch. At one point during our brief rest, I couldn't find my father until I spotted something up in the air on top of a picnic table and realized it was his cycling shoe. He was lying on the table with his leg in the air as he stretched out his tight hamstrings and lower back. He was absolutely determined to continue on! Lunch ended and for a while it looked like the stretching had done the trick.

We made it through the afternoon, and toward the end of the

day, with only a handful of miles left, I saw a sign advertising a local attraction called Pawnee Rock. From 1821 until the late 1800s, Pawnee Rock was a noted landmark along the Sante Fe Trail. I remembered Mike mentioning this historical site as one of the spots that settlers making their way west had used to get their bearings. Thousands of wagons creaked through, and pioneers recorded their impressions of the site in journals and letters.

Despite its historical significance, stopping there was the last thing I wanted to do. I was cold and sore, and because of my father's slow pace, I had been outside in the howling wind far longer than eighty-four miles normally would have required. Then I recalled Barry's advice about taking time to see places you might never have the chance to see again. *At the end of the ride,* I thought, *I won't remember how cold I was or how sore my legs were. I'll remember that I took the road less traveled to experience something new.* I turned in the saddle to make sure my dad was okay and shouted, "I think I'm going ahead to check out this place. Are you going to be okay?" I could barely hear his reply over the wind. Then I saw his thumbs-up sign, so I put some power into Shiva's pedals and sprinted ahead to explore a slice of history.

It was less than a mile off our route. Turning away from the headwind, I encountered a sudden quiet that felt foreign to my senses. I'd grown accustomed to the endless moaning of the wind, and now that it was finally at my back, the stillness seemed eerie. A hill rose up at the end of the silent road, and I pushed Shiva up to a large concrete structure at the top. It was an open building with four thick pillars supporting a viewing platform, and several iron-wrought spiral staircases wound their way up to the top of the structure. I placed Shiva against one of the pillars and awkwardly climbed the black iron steps in my cycling shoes. There wasn't another soul in sight.

When I reached the top, I was greeted by one of the most expansive vistas of land I'd ever seen. Because of the complete lack of elevation in Kansas, I saw farther than I ever thought possible, at least ten miles in every direction. Far off in the distance, cars and trucks with tiny headlights drove along the highways that my father and I had spent a good portion of the day traversing. All around me were stretches of farmland in neat grids, like a patchwork quilt sewn together by generations of care. I could only imagine how this place must have looked during the height of harvest season, with row upon row of straight, proud-looking stalks of corn and mature wheat swaying in the breeze. I snapped a few photos before clambering down the steps.

As I rode away, I felt a sense of fulfillment I hadn't yet experienced on the ride. Previously at the end of each day, I was always satisfied (and often downright surprised) that I'd made it to the motel. That day I'd taken the initiative and gone off of the beaten path to see something I would normally have passed by, especially in those conditions. Granted, the site was only a mound of earth in the middle of the flat Kansas terrain, but it stood for something that resonated deep within me.

Riding swiftly to catch up with my father, I wasn't thinking about how long I'd been in the saddle or how drastically our pace had been reduced. I thought about how difficult it must have been for those pioneer families trying to cross this great country of ours. How much courage does it take to strap all your worldly possessions onto a wagon and risk your life to navigate the perils of untamed plains and mountains? Those settlers certainly hadn't had a nicely paved road to follow, a state-of-the-art bicycle for transportation, or a GPS for guidance. They had only the dream of a better life as they faced disease and unknown terrain so treacherous that it split axles and broke apart wheels. Courage comes in many forms, and it was time for me to chart the course of my life just as those pioneers had charted theirs so many years ago.

When I caught up with my dad, he was on the side of the road once again, but this time, instead of stretching, he was rummaging through his saddlebag, looking for his tire pump. As if riding with an aching back wasn't enough, his tire had gone completely flat. We called for help from the support van, and as we waited, he asked me about Pawnee Rock. I told him I was glad I took the time to visit.

Then I told him I was ready to get out of the wind, and with a big grin, my dad said he was ready too. Then he said something I'll never forget. "Thanks for sticking with me today," he said. "I don't think I would have made it out here without you." I nodded back at my father with a smile. It was an honor to help a man I'd looked up to all my life. "No problem," I said. The shadows were growing very dark as we rode into the motel parking lot, but I didn't care. We had made it and I was proud of my father for sticking it out.

That night, after a hot shower and a good meal, I thought about the day. It had been another challenge, to be sure, but I'd felt things I hadn't felt in a long time—confidence and courage. The first week of the ride had been brutal, filled with unimaginable heat, endless climbs, and chafing to parts of my body I hadn't realized could chafe. Time and time again, I'd questioned my sanity. But after everything I had endured, with the help of my father and my ABB teammates, I was starting to believe in myself again. I may not have been traveling in a covered wagon, but I also was daring to do something few people had ever done.

Demons and Playlists

Day 15: Great Bend, Kansas-Abilene, Kansas
Distance: 129 Miles
Total Distance: 1,593 Miles

STILL DRESSED IN MY PAJAMAS, I HEADED DOWN THE HALLWAY WITH AN empty bucket toward the humming of the ice machine. My dad had gotten up early that morning to stretch out his back, and I thought he might need some ice to reduce the inflammation. By the time I returned with a filled bucket clutched in one hand, he had a towel on the carpeted floor and was finishing a set of stretches with determination. To my surprise, he got up with a broad grin across his face and greeted me with a strong, reassuring hug. "Feeling better today—actually pretty good!" he said.

Seeing him in such high spirits was better than a morning cup of coffee. I returned his grin, all thoughts of the ice bucket forgotten. His positive attitude was infectious, and before I knew it, a tune was playing in my head as I packed my clothes and readied Shiva for another day on the road. I was happy to have my dad back in good riding shape, especially since the days of eighty-mile rides were behind us. We faced more than 120 miles of open highway today across the Kansas landscape on our way to the city of Abilene.

I stripped off my pajamas and selected my outfit for the day. It was cold again that morning, and the gray, overcast sky announced it was planning to stay that way until further notice. Once more I pulled out my cold-weather gear and slipped into the tight-fitting Under Armour. We rode the elevator down to breakfast with a few sleepy cyclists, and a few more were scattered among the tables in the lounge. I loaded my paper plate with the usual motel morning food: powdered eggs, toast from a massive toaster, instant oatmeal, and orange juice from a machine. I crossed the room and joined my father. He ate silently, and I knew that despite his good mood, he had lingering doubts about how his back would hold up during another grueling day on the road. Plunging my fork into the quivering mass of eggs, I was content to share his silence.

I had a lot to on my mind too. I'd started a conversation the previous afternoon with one of my best friends, Brian, and I was still thinking about it. Our friendship went as far back as grade school, and we had spent many hours at each other's houses. Brian called my mother Mama Wags, and Mrs. Drury had been like a second mother to me, offering a warm smile and a delicious meal every time I showed up in her kitchen. Since the start of the ride, the whole Drury family had been an unending source of support and encouragement. On the day after I posted my experience of "standin' on a corner in Winslow, Arizona," Mr. Drury, an accomplished guitar player and songwriter, had sent me an uplifting e-mail about how excited he was for me, especially since we were both such big fans of the Eagles.

During my brief detour to Pawnee Rock, Brian and I had text messaged each other about the difficulties and the rewards of the ride. I told him that the physical rigors were obvious and that while I didn't profess to enjoy riding more than one hundred miles every day, my body was rising to the challenge. I confessed to him that it was my mental energy, though, that was starting to concern me. I admitted to Brian it had been easier in the beginning to stay motivated with personal bests like crossing the biggest mountain, getting through the hottest temperatures, and riding the longest distance. But the farther we rode into the Midwest and the deeper we pressed into the breadbasket of America, the more I struggled to maintain a positive attitude. As soon as I had shared my misgivings with Brian, I felt guilty. I was regretting even hinting at such self-absorption when he texted me back a message that made me pause.

"I was interviewing this woman for my blog, Overcoming Graduation," he wrote. "She is an accomplished Ironman triathlete and has completed several in her life. She told me when you're competing in endurance events, you need to have a really good playlist or be at peace with your demons. If you're not, there's nothing but time out there for you to confront them." It had been powerful advice, but I still needed to get my father safely to the motel after he sent them, so I tucked his words away for another time.

Our conversation returned that morning as I shuffled down the hall to the ice machine. *Demons or a good playlist,* I thought. And by the time I saddled up on Shiva, the conversation was really tugging at me. The playlist comment reminded me of our first day in California when Mike sternly addressed our group about safety on the trip. He was adamant that no music was allowed while riding—not even with speakers attached to the bike without headphones. A few riders had been upset, but the point was nonnegotiable. My iPod, filled with hundreds of songs, was packed deep in my luggage.

With 129 miles of open road ahead of me today, I had plenty of time to ponder the demons that lived inside me. Most of the time they were hidden, but I decided to spend the day giving each a name. But before I could name them, I knew the tougher task would be to actually acknowledge them. They had lived in a part of my mind that had been locked for a very long time, but I knew I was the only one with the key.

I took a deep breath and thought, *Ready or not, here goes.*

Fear. Fear is a hungry mouth gnashing its teeth in the center of my chest. During my worst days, I could feel fear sucking the colors out of the world around me. Fear smacks its lips with relish as my hopes and dreams slide down into its ravenous gullet. When it's not busy chewing on the remains of my courage, fear likes to whisper about all of the things I've done wrong with my life. Then I shatter under the weight of the "what ifs" and the "should haves" of perfect hindsight until I am a million pieces spread across the floor.

Guilt. Guilt has beady little eyes and a greedy, drooling mouth. It runs down the growing list of all the wrong things I've done to the people I love. It knows every birthday dinner, college class, homework assignment, or social event I've ever missed because I was too high, too drunk, or simply too depressed to attend. Guilt is a burning sensation that makes my face turn crimson with heat.

Addiction. In my mind, the addict is an old-fashioned knight in tarnished armor, brandishing a rusted sword. His plated steel once gleamed brightly with polished brilliance and possibility, but the corrosive substances on which he had grown so dependent had worn the warrior down into a diminished version of who he once was. The tarnished knight represents the core values I had once stood for, such as hard work, discipline, honor, and courage, all compromised by addiction. Every time I listened to the silky smooth whispers of my tarnished knight promising that things would be better tomorrow and saying that I should just forget about today, the lie would be back the next morning when nothing ever felt better.

Shame. Shame keeps an account of each time I allowed addiction to have its way and to throw me off track. It does this with a huge book of aging parchment that it carries on its back with chains wrapped around its body. The weight is so great that shame is forced to stay hunched over in a painful position.

Fear, guilt, addiction, and shame enjoyed fighting one another for their rightful place within my mind. There was never any peace as each demon demanded the next audience and haggled over how long it would last. During restless nights alone in my room, I shuddered as the demons circled one another. Training for the bike ride over the past year, I'd done everything in my power to conquer each one and to make my life better. I desperately wanted to understand why I'd allowed them to block out the joy that once was so abundant in my life.

Riding towards the town of Abilene, I thought about the title of my blog, "Leaving It on the Road." For the first time, I believed I had identified exactly what *it* was. My *it* was the collection of my past mistakes along with the weight of a future that no longer seemed to apply to me. *It* was the fear of change and of the unknown. I realized that the demon of fear definitely led the pack and had been with me from the moment I began pedaling away from the Pacific Ocean. It was next to me as I rode up endless mountains and pedaled through desert heat I didn't even know existed. This demon lay beside me at night when I thought about the next day's ride and wondered how I would find the strength to get through it. But each day I had continued to ride. Each day I pushed fear aside and instead leaned on the group for strength when I needed support. I told fear to get lost as I rode into parking lots in the dark, exhausted but triumphant. Each time I fought back, I began to remember what life was like without fear. I also started to feel comfortable with the idea of people leaning on me for support. Since my junior year in college, I hadn't felt I was in a position to be of much use to anyone, and I loved the old familiar feeling of being able to help my family and my friends.

The longer we rode, the more I realized that while I knew I was physically up to the ride, in a moment of clarity, I now understood the importance of the mind-body relationship in the pursuit of goals. Success requires that the mind and the body be in harmony and share a balance. The past two weeks proved I had the body part down, but what about the other half? As each demon occupied a smaller and smaller piece of real estate in my mind, positive and confident emotions began to take up residence.

Every day I left another piece of my *it* on the road. They may have been small pieces, but sometimes that's the best you can do. And eventually, all of those pieces add up.

Food for Thought

Day 16: Abilene, Kansas-Topeka, Kansas
Distance: 108 Miles
Total Distance: 1,701 Miles

THE MORNING WAS OVERCAST WITHOUT THE SUN'S WARMTH TO BREAK the chill, so I zipped my jacket all the way to my chin to retain as much body heat as possible. Gripping Shiva's handlebars tightly, I rode into our now-familiar drafting formation against the Kansas headwinds. I have to admit I wasn't too sad on our last full day of riding through Kansas. Because of the flat terrain, I'd been traveling without changing position in the saddle, and my rear end was protesting.

By noontime, a series of sloping hills appeared on our route, and I gave quiet thanks as I finally stood up on Shiva's pedals. With another nod from the cycling gods, bright patches of warm, buttery sunlight started punching through the dissipating cloud cover. At first only a few pockets of light briefly appeared, but as the day wore on, the pockets lasted longer and longer. Soon scattered pools of light danced playfully across the road all around us. After spending so many days riding into a chilly headwind, I laughed like a child at being in the warm sunshine. I was completely present in the moment as I looked onto each side of the single-lane highway and took in the sights around me.

Every few miles, a red barn on a hill overlooked the pastures

143

below it. Bright emerald grass, lush enough to make a bed on, ran gently up those hills while an occasional cow ambled slowly around the fences, softly mooing in the hushed air. Even the wind had died away, its flow disrupted by the rise and fall of the hills, offering a fresh change in the air as well as a fresh change in the saddle. Since we'd started on our cross-country journey, I'd grown adept at the art of daydreaming to pass the time and to pretend I was anywhere else except on a hundred-mile stretch of desert with no shade in sight. But on that afternoon, no daydreaming was necessary with such beautiful scenery under a sun-drenched sky. I didn't worry about what tomorrow would bring, what would happen when the ride was finished, or whether my dad's back would hold out until we made it to our rest day in Springfield, Illinois.

Instead, I admired how the sunlight made the fields glow and how the breeze carried the scent of crops beginning to grow hardy and firm. The land sustained the families who lived on it and coaxed the soil to produce food for the rest of America. It all reminded me of a simpler time and a slower pace. I marveled at the relationship between the land and the farmers who invested hours of diligence, patience, perseverance, and extremely hard work. I thought of Barry's tour of the farming tool museum in North Dakota and the stories he must have heard from the elderly couple who ran it. Even with modern technology, the effort it took to ensure a healthy crop and a smooth harvest was beyond the scope of my imagination.

Eventually, the farmlands gave way to open fields of white and purple wildflowers and the sweet smell of pollen and nectar flooded my senses. My father also seemed to be enjoying the day, and we slowed our pace to match our moods. We were in no rush to reach our destination, and neither of us wanted to replace the beauty surrounding us with a stark motel room in Topeka.

With more than ninety miles left on our 108-mile ride, I let my mind wander back to the sumptuous feast my fellow riders and I had enjoyed the previous night in Abilene. We'd chosen a restaurant highly recommended by Mike, who assured our group that the service and the food couldn't be beat. From the moment we entered,

I felt inclined to agree with him. The Brookville Hotel reminded me more of an old-style country home than of a restaurant. A large porch gave shelter to approaching visitors in case of rain, and huge picture windows offered views of happy patrons enjoying their meals.

When we walked in, hundreds of knickknacks for sale lined shelves along the lobby wall. The whole house smelled like a good home-cooked meal, flowery potpourri, and scented candles. A young woman behind an old-fashioned wooden desk greeted us warmly. "Table for six?" she asked with a beaming smile. There were indeed six in our group that night—Joe, Max, Jan, Greg, my father, and me. Greg, usually a strong rider who led the pack, had recently slowed his pace because he hadn't been feeling well. As he struggled to keep up with even our usual band of riders in the rear, I tried to keep his mind off of his exhausted legs with some light conversation. Greg was fond of saying, "It is what it is," and exemplified the sentiment by taking his fatigue in stride. I was happy to have him join us for dinner, and it looked like we were all in for a treat as our hostess led us to our table.

I spotted Mike and his wife, Barbara, seated at a table for two. They flashed big, knowing smiles when they saw us approaching. Taking my seat, I glimpsed another table of hungry ABB cyclists, all listening eagerly to their waitress as she explained the way things worked at the restaurant. "It's a family-style dinner," she said, "with a fixed menu of options." I noticed that on our table were sets of gleaming silverware and delicate blue-patterned china pieces, but no menus graced the white linen tablecloths. "There will be a main course of fried chicken, breasts and wings, with sides of mashed potatoes, green beans, cornbread, and cranberry sauce." The waitress continued listing the food selections with practiced ease. When she finally ended her list—"topped off with a brownie fresh from the oven with a scoop of vanilla ice cream"—I thought I'd died and gone to heaven. All speech fled my brain, and I could only gape and drool as she finished taking their drink orders and made her way over to us.

As the waitress finished explaining things to the six of us, large platters of food began appearing at our neighboring table. I was all but frothing at the mouth and almost missed my cue to order something to drink. "Chocolate milk?" I asked in a small, hopeful voice. I dared to believe this place might have my favorite beverage. The waitress nodded with a smile and jotted down my order. My heart swelled. This restaurant was turning out to be a paradise for our hungry and well-traveled group.

Before long, those same platters of steaming food were served to our table and the restaurant was filled with the sounds of knives clattering and forks scraping across china. As our family-style meal continued to appear in waves by the well-dressed staff, I couldn't devour the food fast enough. The flavors, the scents, and the sheer volume of food were overwhelming. And everything was delicious! The chicken was moist and tasty. The mashed potatoes were creamy with butter, and when I added a river of gravy from the ornate gravy boat, no words could describe the happiness I felt. *This must have been what it was like back in the days of fresh-churned butter and garden-grown potatoes*, I mused as I covered yet another potato mound.

Each time we finished off a platter, another took its place. I wanted to sample every morsel the table offered, and I did. To my surprise and delight, one of my favorite side dishes turned out to be creamed corn. It was the first time I'd tried the dish, and although I couldn't tell you if it was made only from cream and corn, I can tell you it tasted wonderfully sweet. Every time I felt like I couldn't manage one more bite, I somehow found another helping of food on the plate in front of me that I just couldn't stand wasting. Our waitress stayed right on point with my chocolate milk, too. My frosted mug never ran empty.

I didn't think it would be humanly possible to make room for dessert, but after empty plates and gravy-stained napkins had been cleared, I sat back and eyed the incoming ice cream–soaked brownie with the same look of determination I used against hills and mountains. I am proud to say that I conquered yet another summit!

By the time we finished our epic dinner, everyone at the table was sitting back with a content smile and a loosened belt. Our meal had been an overwhelming success, and we expressed our appreciation to all involved at the restaurant. Sleep was easy to come by that night, and the last thing I remember thinking was, *If we could have a feast like that at the end of every day on the road, we could make it all the way to the East Coast with no problem at all!*

Roads Left Behind, Roads Yet to Cover

Day 17: Topeka, Kansas-Cameron, Missouri
Distance: 123 Miles
Total Distance: 1,824 Miles

I JOINED THE OTHER RIDERS ALONG THE MISTY STREETS OF TOPEKA around seven in the morning. About eight miles down the road, the fog was so dense that we almost missed Mike's lean figure flagging us down next to the gleaming ABB support van glinting through thick, swirling clouds of vapor. I looked down at the road where Mike was pointing, and in large capital letters spray-painted in white on the blacktop, I saw a simple statement without punctuation: OFFICIAL ABB FAST AM ½ WAY POINT.

Mike had painted a large dot underneath the words with an arrow pointing directly at it so there was no confusion about where the halfway point was located. Looking around at the group, I was filled with an immense sense of accomplishment and pride. We swiftly organized into a rough semicircle around the dot and, after a few minutes of shuffling and adjusting, arranged ourselves into two neat rows across the road. The taller riders stood in the back while the shorter ones, including my dad and me, got down on one knee. We didn't spend too much time posing for photographs, because the day was still young and we had more than one hundred miles to cover. I did, however, get a nice shot of Phil kneeling triumphantly with me over the halfway marker. The fact that the ride was already halfway done was hard to believe. Even though there were still roughly 1,700 miles left until we reached the Atlantic Ocean, the days seemed to be flying by. We were averaging 115 miles a day, and that still blew my mind whenever I thought about it. In addition to celebrating our halfway point, my dad and I celebrated the fact that he was no longer experiencing back pain.

Later that day as we left the gently rolling pastures of eastern Kansas behind, a sign welcomed us into the seventh state of our journey, Missouri. My father was feeling so good that he decided to stretch his legs with some of the faster riders. As usual, I was content to keep up my steady but slower pace and soon found myself sharing the road with our mechanic, Jim. We had ridden together a few times in recent days during his time off from the support van. Often, we met up when the rest of the riders had gone ahead, leaving me to once again bring up the rear. It didn't bother me at all anymore to be at the very back of the pack and to arrive last at SAG stops and motel parking lots. The ride had taught me to let go of my ego-driven indignation at being smoked every day by riders who had thirty or more years on me in the saddle. This day was no different as I simply enjoyed the sunshine that had burned away the clammy morning mist and had warmed up the rolling Missouri hillsides.

Not long after we met up, Jim and I encountered several tough climbs. As we shifted our gears, he began talking to me about some of the special people he'd met during his years with ABB and about how he liked to drop in on them when his route brought him close to their homes. He mentioned his favorite bar, Bud's Place in Little Falls, New York. He stopped by every time he was in the area, and I imagined him in a scene from *Cheers* "where everybody knows your name." I listened to his deep, gravelly voice, happy for the conversation. I enjoyed the solitude in the back of the pack, but I didn't mind exchanging thoughts and stories with someone every now and then.

We rode under a thick canopy of green leaves over the road. The sun had come out in full force, so the shade and the cool breeze felt nice across my sweaty brow. When Jim finished talking, I confided in him that now that we were halfway done with the ride, I was a little nervous about what my life would be like once I got back to New Jersey. I didn't share the depth of my uncertainty, but I hinted at wondering how I'd feel after accomplishing such a massive undertaking. Jim listened patiently to my concerns, a thoughtful expression crossing his weathered face. His cheeks and the strip of his forehead not covered by his helmet still boasted a deep crimson hue from the desert's touch. I could tell Jim was mulling over what I'd said, because after a few miles, he spoke with the slow, thoughtful tone of someone with plenty of experience.

"A lot of guys on these rides ask those same types of questions," he said. "I see them thinking about it as the end day gets closer. I've kept in touch with some of them, and a few started to feel a little lost, a little directionless, when they got back home."

I said nothing as I waited for him to continue. Those thoughts had been cropping up in my head ever since we'd left the halfway point. The past eight months had been dedicated to training to ride Shiva across the United States with my father. Period. I'd gotten up each morning with one thought dominating every move and decision I made. When I ate, I thought about what kinds of fuel would best help me train. When I worked out with weights, I thought about which muscle groups were most important for the hills I'd encounter. When I did a spin class, I thought about how sprinting in the saddle would help my endurance. As I trained in my basement, watching Forrest Gump save Lieutenant Dan or James Bond blow up another car in *Casino Royale*, I thought about how an extra hour of riding would help me achieve my goal. Where would that leave me once my mission was done and I returned to the so-called real world?

Jim continued talking, seemingly unaware of how closely I was following his every word. "When riders talk to me about it, I tell them it's natural to have those feelings," he said. "They just accomplished something that very few people can even imagine, let alone actually do on their own free will." He cocked one eye at me while keeping the other on the road ahead. "I tell them that they need to find something else, another adventure they can focus on. It doesn't have to be right away, but when those feelings of restlessness come up, I found a new goal can really help."

The road had been empty for miles at that point, and I rode alongside Jim as we climbed slope after slope together. Once again, a conversation with one of my new friends had given me great comfort. I knew that every journey had a beginning and an end, but that didn't mean that the spirit of adventure would disappear. Who knew what other roads were left to cover in my life? Rather than being nervous, I felt excited at the prospect.

That night at RAP, Mike told us that we should expect a few changes in terrain the next few days. "The days of flat Kansas prairies are over, gentlemen," he explained, with a mischievous smile on his face. "Tomorrow it's going to get a bit hilly on our route." We all looked at each other. Apparently they didn't nickname Missouri the Land of a Thousand Hills for nothing.

Land of a Thousand Hills

Day 18: Cameron, Missouri-Kirksville, Missouri
Distance: 119 Miles
Total Distance: 1,943 Miles

MY FATHER, JOE, AND I WARMED UP OUR MUSCLES ALONG TEN MILES
of deserted country road before reaching Highway 36. The morning
sky appeared dark and heavy with the threat of showers. A few times
the sun tried to peek past some of the less stubborn storm clouds,
but the clouds won each time and I anticipated a brief shower or two.
Beads of sweat formed along the bridge of my nose as I struggled to
loosen my stiff legs. I was sure that the burning pain in my thighs
had been a parting gift from the seemingly endless series of climbs
and descents toward the end of the previous day. From the way Mike
had described this day's route, I knew it was only a matter of time
before Missouri's roads became even more challenging. It was the
eighteenth day of our trip, and my father and I had a comfortable
routine: wake up, eat, ride, eat, ride, snack, ride, eat, stretch, shower,
sleep, and repeat. We did our best each morning to be prepared for
the road, but once we left the motel parking lot, it was anybody's
guess what the day would bring.

I tried shaking off my discomfort to enjoy some of the sights and
sounds around me. Early morning on the back roads of Missouri has
a lot to offer. Life seemed to be bursting from every crack and seam
in the asphalt. Flowers of all shapes and colors were blossoming

along the road among taller, hardier tufts of grass. I breathed deeply and took in the heavy smell of mulch and fertilizer mixed with the earthy tones of freshly cut grass.

I couldn't help but feel a little bit homesick. As soon as the weather grew warm back in New Jersey and the grass began growing in earnest, I'd be outside on early Saturday mornings, steadily walking behind our red lawn mower. We have a big yard, so for the better part of the morning and the afternoon, I'd go back and forth on the green grass while listening to music through my headphones. Each time I emptied a large bag of freshly cut grass into the woods at the back of our house, the same earthly scent filled my nose with its heady aroma.

Thankfully, the early morning hills were gentle, and I rarely had to shift Shiva's gears to crest their summits. We came across a sturdy-looking cobblestone bridge over a churning river, swollen from recent spring rains. The bridge radiated a certain ageless quality, and the journalist in me couldn't help but question its past. Could this bridge have been an important crossing point for troops during the Civil War? Perhaps this crossing had been a link in the Underground Railroad as slaves risked everything for freedom and equality. Several other scenarios were playing out in my mind until we rounded the corner and I caught my first glimpse of the real hills of Missouri. They were still in the distance, but I saw several of them lined up in an orderly row and I conjured the image of a wild roller coaster. I rolled my neck to loosen my shoulders, took a few long sips of water, and got ready for our first true climb of the day. Gone were the graceful rises and falls of the morning. It was time for the big leagues.

The first hill loomed in front of us, and I frantically dropped Shiva's resistance to make it up the steep incline. The three of us climbed and climbed, our legs spinning furiously while we powered up the first slope. My legs finally had shed their soreness and I was feeling strong and limber. Coasting down the backside of the hill, I was immediately confronted by the next climb. After so many days on the flats of Kansas, it felt good to climb and I attacked each hill with ferocity, relishing the challenge as the blood pumped through my legs. I felt a sense of satisfaction that comes with being fully invested in the moment.

Every climb to the summit brought a descent. As I flew down each hill, the world picked up speed and flowed past me in streaks of green and brown. When the descent was over, my heart would be left racing, and I would eagerly throw myself into the next hill rising above me. I stopped counting the hills we had climbed after fifty and I heard Mike's voice echoing in my head: "Some cyclists who pass through here like to call this state Mi-ser-y," he joked in his Alabama drawl. "You'll see what I mean soon enough."

Despite the damp cold, sweat poured down my face. Up and down we pedaled and then up and down some more. It didn't take me long to realize that my climbing strategy wasn't working very well. I thought I was an expert at climbing. Hadn't I conquered the towering mountains in New Mexico and Arizona and everything in between? Yet, by the time we reached our SAG lunch, I was exhausted. My leg muscles trembled with fatigue as I sat back in one of the folding chairs scattered around the gravel lot. At the rate I was burning up energy, it wouldn't be long before I was totally tapped out. There were plenty more hills ahead. How was I going to make it through this roller coaster of a state? My answer came soon enough.

As I ate what was arguably one of the biggest lunches I've ever had—two huge turkey sandwiches, two bananas, four granola bars, and several big fistfuls of mixed nuts—Richard sat down beside me. Usually, he rode with George, and we'd see the two of them only at breakfast or RAP. One of Richard's quads had been bothering him over the past few days, and he was taking it easy by carefully pacing himself through the hills. It was becoming well known that if you were sick, hurt, tired, or just felt like taking it easy, you could always find company with Ralph, Eric, and Joe at the back of the pack. We were like the Statue of Liberty of the cycling world; we welcomed everyone.

We finished our lunches together, and when it was time to leave, Richard decided to stay in the back with our little group of three.

After a few miles pedaling up and down another series of hills, I noticed Richard closely eyeing my cadence, his tanned forehead scrunched tightly in concentration. I felt horribly exposed and vulnerable, as if I'd been caught breaking some kind of unknown draconian cycling law.

Finally, he looked up and smiled at me. "You're working too hard," he said. "Why don't you try shifting your gears to a lighter setting?" Confused, I looked down at my gears and then up at the looming hills ahead of us. "What do you mean?" I asked.

"Keeping those gears at such a high resistance level will only waste energy in the long run," he explained. "The key is to conserve your strength and use the gears to your advantage. Drop them down and spin your way up to the top. On the way down the hill, crank up that resistance to add speed to your downward momentum. Let gravity do the work. Then you can coast up farther on the next climb. Remember, Eric—you want to ride smarter, not harder."

I nodded in agreement. What he was telling me made perfect sense. Instead of trying to stubbornly force my way up each hill, wasting my strength, I could use Shiva's gears and the gravity of each downward slope to my advantage. The old method might have worked with smaller hills or if there had been fewer climbs to attack, but not in this endless steeply rolling terrain.

I followed Richard's advice as we hit the next slope, steadily dropping Shiva's gears. The reduced effort was immediately apparent, and as we continued climbing, my legs felt less strained. I bumped up the resistance at the top of the hill and flew down the backside so fast that I made it almost halfway up the next climb before putting any pressure on the pedals. What a difference! My smile matched Richard's, and he stayed with me for quite a while, advising and encouraging me every few miles and helping get me through one of the toughest days since Dalhart. Without his sound advice, the rest of the afternoon would have been much harder.

Toward the end of the day, Richard went ahead and George pedaled up beside us. His visit didn't last long, though, and before I knew it, he took off like a bullet until he became a powder-blue speck in the distance. The sight of George's seemingly effortless sprint away from the rest of us sorry sacks stirred the competitive spirit within me. I wasn't going to let him get away that easily, and without a word to Joe or my dad, I sprinted hard after George's swiftly departing figure. The stale afternoon air felt fresher as I picked up my pace and gathered speed beneath Shiva's wheels. *Faster! Faster!* I urged my weary legs, and before long, I felt stirrings of joy beneath my layers of exhaustion.

But no matter how hard I rode, George was always at least two hills ahead of me. Whenever I crested a hill, his diminishing form would already be slipping behind the next one, but I didn't care. I felt no frustration or anger, just the simple joy of the chase. I finally let George disappear over the horizon and, panting hard, slowed Shiva. I'd assumed I was alone, but when I turned around I saw that Joe was right behind me. Though he was breathing heavily and his brow glistened with sweat, he smiled triumphantly. "I knew I could catch you!" he exuberantly exclaimed. *Catch me?* I regarded Joe with confusion, but he quickly explained that, like me, he'd wanted to break out of the weariness that had seemed to settle over everyone during the afternoon. "When I saw you chasing George, I decided to chase you."

He'd kept at it, and as I slowed down, finally letting George go, he sped up, seeing his chance to catch me. Then he told me that my father was chasing him! It hadn't been my intention to inspire a good old-fashioned chase, but sure enough, I had. My father appeared a few minutes later, breathing heavily but with a big smile on his face. "You guys trying to ditch me?" he asked jokingly. Sometimes the unplanned moments in life really are the best.

Two hours later we all pulled into our next stop in the town of Kirksville. At RAP that night, one of the guys claimed that he'd counted more than 250 summits and Mike informed us we had climbed a total of 6,800 feet. Throw in our impromptu chase scene, and I was more than ready to call it a day.

The Wolf Pack

Day 19: Kirksville, Missouri-Quincy, Illinois
Distance: 95 Miles
Total Distance: 2,038 Miles

IN JUST A FEW MORE HOURS, THE ABB TEAM FINALLY WOULD SAY GOOD-bye to Mi-ser-y forever. That afternoon we'd board a barge on the muddy banks of the Mississippi River with our faithful bikes and our gear in tow and cross over to Illinois. We'd be traveling only ninety-five miles this day, although how long that would take, considering we weren't out of Missouri yet, was anyone's guess. *Yes*, I thought wearily, *a short day in the saddle would be most welcome.* Maybe if we got to the motel at a reasonable hour, I could catch up on my blog or correspond with the people who'd been following my progress across the country.

My dad and I walked our bikes downstairs to the parking lot, where the rest of the ABB riders were milling about. Long gone were the days when I had to rely on nametags clipped to saddlebags. Although a few riders were less familiar than others, I'd grown to enjoy everyone's company very much. For the past several days, Barry had decided to drop back and hang out with Joe, my dad, and me. I always felt like the four of us fit perfectly, though I could never quite figure out what made us so compatible. We just seemed to belong together.

I don't know exactly when I got the inspiration to give our

little group of four the unofficial nickname of the Wolf Pack, but I do remember how I came up with it. My dad made an offhand comment one day about how we were always chasing the rest of the group. Wolves are pack animals, and during a hunt, they can run miles and miles to bring down their prey. I told my dad that if it wasn't for my own cycling pack, I doubted I'd survive. That was all it took, and it wasn't long before the nickname the Wolf Pack caught on with my dad and Joe. Because Barry didn't spend all his time in the back with us, we made him an honorary member. Word of our new title spread throughout the group, and it wasn't unusual for riders to yell, "Hey, it's the Wolf Pack!" as they passed us by.

There was another reason I decided to give our group a name. During the first few days of the ride, I was wracked with frustration and borderline disbelief as men twice my age flew by me on the road. They'd rise every morning before the sun and eat up the miles. The first few days I'd been burning to hang with the faster riders and show them what a young guy like me could do. It took me less than three days to understand that my ego-driven riding style was completely unrealistic. Even at my maximum effort, I was still spending more time on the road than almost anyone else. If I went too hard at the start of the ride, I was going to burn myself out before the end of the first week. It had been a bitter pill to swallow to realize that at no time would I ever lead our group unless all the other cyclists spontaneously burst their tires and/or lost their bike chains.

Before I came up with the Wolf Pack, something had been missing from my rear-guard status—an identity. So instead of feeling embarrassed by my slowness, I turned my perceived weakness into something to celebrate. My dad, Joe, and I took to howling from the seats of our bicycles. When I was tired and sore, I would imagine the rest of the bikers as fleet-footed deer bounding ahead of me, too nimble to be caught. A wolf never gives up on a chase when it's hunting because if it does, the whole pack starves. And a wolf never lets its pack down, and I knew I couldn't either.

A few hours before we reached the Mississippi River, we took a short SAG stop in a small country town. A dilapidated building served as our backdrop, with broken glass filling the mostly empty windowpanes. Mike explained that the place had been a hotel for travelers and railroad workers in what was once a bustling railroad community. In that eerie, almost haunting atmosphere, I loaded up my salty granola bars and sweet-tasting bananas as I scanned the silent hotel. When I was younger, I loved watching documentaries on the supernatural like *Scariest Places on Earth* and *Ghost Hunters*. The abandoned hotel would have been perfect on either show. Part of me believed that if I acted as if I wasn't paying attention, a ghostly silhouette might stare at me from one of the empty windows.

It looked like the gray day would soon give way to rain, so I pulled my neon-yellow raincoat from the elastic back pockets of my jersey and bundled up against the coming downpour. We still had a good way to travel from the SAG stop before we reached our big river crossing, and I wanted to stay as dry as possible. Evidence of rain was apparent in the soggy meadows and the pools of still water that had collected in divots along the muddy road. Thick pockets of mud oozed under our tires as we rode.

When at last we arrived at the Mississippi River crossing, we were greeted by a surprise from Barbara. Set up alongside the river was our SAG lunch. As my dad, Joe, and I signed in and washed our hands, Barbara informed us that other than Greg, we were the last ones to catch the boat. I had heard that Greg wasn't feeling well, so we decided to stick around until he showed up. Looking down at the spread of food Barbara had laid out, I regretted my earlier pit stop at a gas station. I'd been ravenous and the thought of riding another mile without getting something in my stomach was incomprehensible, so I'd wolfed down a personal pan pizza.

As my dad and Joe enjoyed the food, I sat in a lawn chair and looked across the slow-moving water. My whole life, I'd heard and read about the length and the power of the Mississippi, and it was amazing to see the river up close. Greg's familiar form slowly rode into view, and it didn't take an expert to realize that something was bothering him. He flashed us a weary grin as he dismounted, admitting that he wasn't feeling well. He was determined to keep going, though, and together we took the barge across the Big Muddy.

My cycling shoes were so encased in muck from the riverbank that I knew I'd need a good amount of time to scrape it all off when we got to the other side. If I didn't, I'd risk falling into the road should one of my shoes slip free from the pedal. I had one hand securely on Shiva the whole time, but the water was relatively smooth and free of waves or strong currents, which made the ride enjoyable. When we reached the other side, I stamped my feet against the metal surface of the barge, kicking away any loose mud that might have clung to the bottoms of my shoes. But the river has two banks and there was just as much mud on the other side. Sighing, I slipped my way with Shiva toward drier ground with a fresh coating of mud clinging to her chain and to my cleats.

While banging my shoes yet again against a loose boulder, I watched my father slog his way through the muck. He waited as Joe and Greg slowly made their way through the same ankle-deep sludge and I scouted ahead to check out our newest state of the trip, Illinois. My wish for fewer hills had definitely been answered, but in their place was a headwind of shocking ferocity. With nothing to block its path, it rushed toward us as we cycled past the silos and the refineries that dotted the land. Sometimes it was all I could do to keep moving forward. Luckily, George volunteered to lead the group, so my dad and I sheltered behind his powder-blue jersey.

On the way to our motel in Quincy, I saw houses lining the riverbank that looked like they would belong in any other neighborhood, with one glaring difference: they were on stilts! Whoever had constructed them had kept the seasonal flooding in mind, because each house sat on four stout support pillars that kept it high over the water. Some had stairs starting at ground level that climbed to the front door, while others had boats tied securely to docks beneath. *Just in case they need to borrow a cup of sugar*, I thought. I even spied several mailboxes along the road that were simply labeled "Flood Mail."

By the time we pulled into the motel parking lot, I was ready to get out of the saddle. We had climbed dozens more hills, biked through rain and mud, eaten outside a haunted hotel, crossed the mighty Mississippi, and seen houses built on stilts. All in all, it was a pretty eventful day for the Wolf Pack.

Quiet Heroes

Day 20: Quincy, Illinois-Springfield, Illinois
Distance: 106 Miles
Total Distance: 2,144 Miles

JUST BEFORE MIDNIGHT I WOKE UP WITH TERRIBLE STOMACH CRAMPS. The aching had grown so bad that by one o'clock, I was curled into a ball in the middle of my mattress, gasping for what little air I could force into my painfully tight diaphragm. As I lay in quiet agony, I eventually pinned the source of my discomfort on the questionably fresh personal pizza I'd bought at the gas station the day before. *I'm going to die from a slice of pizza! I knew I should have just sucked it up and waited until the SAG lunch,* I thought. Never trust a pizza with a bit of a tang to it that's been sitting under a warming lamp for who knows how long.

My father slumbered in his bed beside me, gently snoring, yet I felt he was a million miles away. Although he'd never complain about me waking him in the middle of the night, I knew he needed his rest, so I decided not to disturb him while I writhed in pain. A few times, I was sure the ferocity and the volume of my belching would wake him, but he slept right through it. I dozed fitfully, and by morning my situation hadn't improved at all. In fact, my stomach and my overall attitude were worse than ever. When my dad awoke and saw me hunched over the side of my bed, he suggested I try to eat something. I could only glance at him with a haggard expression.

Body language can speak louder than words, and my signs were definitely in the negative.

I looked at my cycling clothes hanging from the towel rack in the bathroom and thought about putting them on. I didn't even have the strength to try, and if I couldn't do that, I surely didn't have the strength to ride 106 miles. I was afraid that if I waited one moment longer to tell my dad I wasn't going to ride, I might change my mind and force myself to pedal until my eventual demise.

Since the beginning of the ride, I'd been all about pushing— pushing my fears aside, pushing the pedals down, pushing myself out of my comfort zone, and pushing myself to finish what I'd set out to do, "come hell or high water," as my grandma Mary used to say. In the past, whenever I made what I thought was a self-indulgent decision, I'd be overwhelmed with negative emotions. Whether it was skipping a training ride or eating a slice of cake, I'd berate myself. But that morning I decided there would be no more pushing. I was simply all pushed out.

"I think I'm going to sit today out," I said, my teeth clenched against the taste of bile. "I'm really not feeling well." I braced myself to feel overwhelmed as usual with guilt and shame. Strangely, my mind was quiet. "I'm sorry you don't feel well," my father replied, looking at me with concern.

When I reached the parking lot dressed in my street clothes, I felt like an intruder at an exclusive party. At Mike's request, everybody on the team was wearing matching red-white-and-blue ABB jerseys. Carefully weaving through the riders loading their luggage into the blue trailer, I walked Shiva over to Mike, who was standing on top of one of the support vans. I quietly repeated what I'd told my dad, searching his lined face for signs of disapproval. I had no doubt that this military man was used to pushing himself to the limits of his capabilities, and the last thing I wanted was to be found lacking in my ride leader's eyes. But if Mike disapproved of my decision, I certainly couldn't tell. He reached down, took Shiva from my grip, and gently secured her in one of the racks. For a moment our gazes met, and I sensed he understood the situation. I knew I wasn't the first guy to need a day off during this trip, and I was sure I wouldn't be the last before Mike's career was over.

"Maybe you'll be out there later this afternoon," he offered as he finished tightening the straps around Shiva's silver frame. "We can keep your cycling stuff in the van if you change your mind." I appreciated his hopeful attitude, but his words of encouragement fell on deaf ears as more bile rose in my throat at the mere thought of riding.

Some of the faster guys had already hit the road as I buckled myself into the backseat of the van. Mike slipped into the driver's seat, fired up the ignition, and slowly followed the cyclists out of the motel parking lot. I stared out of the window at the passing scenery. All I had to do for the next few hours was sit. The thought brought me a slight sense of agitation, but deep down I knew I was making the right call.

That day of all days, there was a special breakfast surprise waiting for everyone fourteen miles down the road at a charming little diner called Mike's Place. The night before as I uncomfortably sat through our RAP meeting, I'd listened as Mike joked that the restaurant was his and that ABB was something he did on the side. I'd managed a slight, tired smile. I always appreciated Mike's efforts to bring humor and lighthearted banter into our RAPs, especially after a long day or difficult conditions on the road. Whether it was nasty weather, the status of a road, or a rider's physical condition, he had an uncanny knack for saying the right thing at the right time. Often, it was a simple word of encouragement, a joke, or a history lesson about the area. In Dodge City he had donned a cowboy hat and silver spurs that jangled from clips attached to the heels of his sneakers.

When we pulled into the small gravel parking lot at Mike's Place, a few familiar bike frames were already leaning up against the side of the cozy-looking restaurant. I followed Mike inside and saw that most of the riders were already seated. With everyone dressed in official ABB jerseys, my previous sensation of being the odd man out returned twofold. My father hadn't made it to the diner yet, so

I found a seat at a small table away from the other guys and stared at a menu. None of the many choices looked appealing given the rolling tide in my stomach.

Several riders noticed my street clothes and asked if I was feeling all right. I answered each concerned question with a lackluster shake of my head, and within minutes our team doctor was on the case. Jan asked me what my symptoms were, and I told him I had no appetite, my stomach was tight with cramps, and I felt bile creep into my mouth every time I burped. "You should take something for that," Big Tom called out from his table. "I used Zantac a few days ago when my stomach was acting up." Jan nodded, saying it sounded like a case of sour stomach. What relief I felt. *Maybe I won't die from a slice of pizza, after all*, I thought. I thanked both men and watched Big Tom dig into his breakfast with gusto. I remembered him folded up on the floor of the firehouse during our SAG lunch outside Albuquerque. He'd been feeling sick to his stomach but was back in the saddle after a day or two.

Another teammate said there was a convenience store across the street. I perked up with interest; surely it would have the medicine I needed. My face flushed from all the attention I was getting from my concerned friends, and when Jim's wife, Jane, who was visiting the group for a few days, drove across the road to buy it for me, I was touched at her generosity. I sheepishly thanked her as I grabbed the package of Zantac, immediately taking a dose with the water on the table. I still wasn't hungry, so I ordered a few pieces of dry toast and some tea and asked for another glass of water.

As the orders came streaming from the kitchen, I could only look on with a tinge of envy as my teammates enjoyed fresh eggs, pancakes, bacon, and hash browns. Of all the days for me to be feeling nauseous! After so many mornings of powdered eggs, a local, farm-raised breakfast would have been wonderful. When it was time to leave, my father said he would stay with me if I wanted him to, but I assured him I would be okay.

When Jim asked if I'd like to ride to the motel with Jane instead of being cooped up in the back of the support van, I jumped at the opportunity. While the riders saddled up, I quickly grabbed my backpack from the van and joined Jane in the front seat of her car. It was a newer model with a built-in GPS that offered an estimated time of arrival as well as directions. I stared at the device with unmasked surprise. We would be arriving at the hotel hours before the rest of the group caught up with us.

This was the first time I'd been in the front seat of a car since my mother had driven us to the airport back in April. I marveled at the speed and ease with which we traveled. Although the ABB support vans were tough and dependable, they weren't designed to break any speed records. I hadn't traveled this fast in a long time, and it was a strangely exhilarating feeling as my body adjusted to the car's speed. There was no wind to fight, no extreme heat or cold, no aches and pains. I occasionally glanced out of the window at the swiftly changing scenery rushing past while Jane drove. She hadn't turned on the radio, and I had forgotten how quiet it could be traveling in a car. On the bike I heard the wind moaning, the birds chirping, and the whisper of tall grass bending against the breeze while leaves rustled overhead. In the car there was nothing to hear beside the steady hum of the engine.

We began talking to pass the time. Jane told me about how she and Jim had fallen in love and eventually gotten married. They had known each other all their lives, she explained, growing up as next-door neighbors in Iowa. When they had decided to get married, it hadn't come as much of a surprise to anyone. They were a couple who seemed to fit together perfectly from the start. We talked about Jim's past adventures as well as their plans for future ones. Not only was Jim a nice guy (I will always be grateful for how he saved me with his generous gift of butt paste during my first few chafed days on the road), but he also had a thirst for adventure that I greatly admired.

At one point during their marriage, Jim had decided he was going to hike the Appalachian Trail from start to finish, a feat known as a thru-hike. Spanning fourteen states, the trail is one of the longest continuously marked footpaths in the world. It runs roughly 2,180 miles from Georgia all the way to Maine and about eighteen hundred to two thousand people attempt the thru-hike each year. It usually takes about six months to complete, but Jim finished his thru-hike in four. During that time, he was given the trail name Jenks.

As Jane spoke, it was easy to see the deep love that this couple had for each other. Not only had they been married longer than I had been alive, but they possessed compassion and generosity for others that touched me deeply. They never hesitated to help those in need. Every year in Iowa there was a bicycle race called the Ragbrai. For seven days cyclists of all ages would ride about sixty-seven miles each day through the countryside. People would camp, ride together, and make new friends during the 450-mile trip. Jim and Jane's house happened to be located near the route that the cyclists traveled, so for a week they opened their doors to the riders. Whether it was a place to sleep, some water or Gatorade, or just to use the bathroom, Jim and Jane were always happy to offer what they could to help others. Bikers would often camp out on their lawn or crash on their couch.

Jim also coached wrestling. He was always volunteering his time and energy, providing guidance and advice to the young men on his team. He strived to be the best mentor he could, and Jane told me that there had been more than a few occasions when a troubled young wrestler had spent a few nights at their house while things cooled off at home.

Jane was no different. She told me that in her free time, she liked to join mission teams traveling to Africa to help those less fortunate. During those visits, she developed close relationships with several of the young children in the villages she aided, continuing to keep in touch through pen pal relationships. Recently she had sent money to a family so they could purchase a goat that provided them with milk and cheese.

Jim and Jane were what I liked to call quiet heroes. They weren't movie stars saving an indigenous people, or big-name politicians trying to stop global warming. They were two average people determined to be as kind and generous to others as they were to each other. They didn't act that way to gain money, power, or fame. They helped those less fortunate than themselves simply because they knew that it was the right thing to do. My own grandmother was a perfect example of a quiet hero. She had been a nurse for fifty years and had poured her heart into caring for men, women, and children. My mother, who believed that the media should focus more on the good in people and not always on the bad, had written a wonderful book about my grandmother titled *Treasures of a Nurse's Heart: My Mother's Memoirs of Love and Wisdom for Everyday Life*.

Growing up, one of my favorite pastimes was diving into comic books filled with heroes in capes and masks, all striving to hand out justice and to lead by example. I often dreamed about what it would be like to don a superhero's mask and to make the world a better place. Listening to Jane, I wondered just how many quiet heroes in my life I had never noticed. I knew now that it wasn't the larger-than-life characters in the comics whom I should be emulating but the quiet heroes who lived among us and made a difference—the ones without the masks and the capes.

Riding across the country with my teammates, I had listened to their stories of inner strength and of selfless giving. Their experiences had given me courage when I felt I had none left. Could I do the same thing for others? Was there a chance I could become a quiet hero? For the first time in my life, I thought that maybe I could.

The miles flew by and we reached the motel well before noon. I thanked Jane for the ride once more as I retrieved my laptop from the back of the car. After she drove away, I checked into the motel and made my way to the room. I dropped headfirst onto the bed closest to the window, thinking it's not the public acts of courage that define each of us but the silent choices we make within ourselves every day.

My father with Matthew and me on vacation. No Man Left Behind!

Almost one third of the way!

The wall.

Facing 40 mph winds on my way to Dalhart, TX.

Reaching Kansas by van instead of bicycle.

Barry was a constant source of inspiration and humor.

Celebrating my father's birthday.

The best meal of the ride.

Pawnee Rock.

Officially half way home!

Welcome to Mi-ser-y.

These roads look more like roller coasters than highways.

Meet the Wolf Pack.

Crossing the mighty Mississippi.

East

Riding a bicycle is the closest
you can get to flying.

—Robin Williams

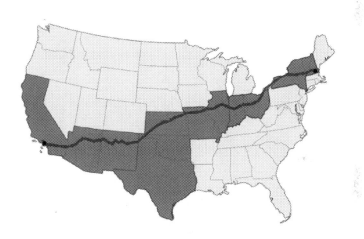

Shifting Gears

Day 22: Springfield, Illinois-Tuscola, Illinois
Distance: 77 Miles
Total: 2,221 Miles

AFTER PLENTY OF SLEEP, SEVERAL GALLONS OF WATER, A WELL-DESERVED two-hour massage, and a few hearty meals, I was anxious to get Shiva back on the road. There were no more rest days on the third and final leg of our journey until we reached our destination—the shores of the Atlantic Ocean in Amesbury, Massachusetts. There was no stopping us now!

Mike had decided to set our loading time for eight in the morning— an hour later than usual because there were only seventy-seven miles before we reached our next stop in Illinois. Though I was excited about returning to the road, I sure hadn't minded the extra sleep. After breakfast, we all wheeled our bikes through the lobby out into the brisk morning air. The winds had calmed down, the sun was drenching every available surface with golden light, and the sky had taken on one of the deepest shades of blue I'd ever seen. It deserved its own crayon color.

I watched my father fidget with the arm and leg warmers he'd put on earlier that morning. The thick sleeves were designed to easily slip on and off moving arms and legs and were ideal for cool mornings that gave way to warm afternoons. I was thankful he'd picked up a pair for me too, because mine were already keeping me warm against the chilly temperatures.

Mike had mentioned during RAP that we'd be passing through a few "old money" areas, and he was right. Riding out of Springfield, we pedaled through some of the most beautiful neighborhoods I had ever seen. The houses were classical Victorians in vibrant shades of pink, purple, and blue with turrets rising high above the streets below. Thick patches of dark green ivy climbed stately walls, and spacious, inviting porches wrapped around each first floor. Towering oak trees loomed over the immaculate sidewalks, providing my father, Joe, and me with ample shade.

Once we were out of the neighborhoods, the road opened up, offering a view of a sprawling rural countryside. Fields of alfalfa and fledgling crops of wheat stretched all the way to the horizon. Sprouting buds teeming with life emerged from the ordered rows, and all signs pointed toward spring. The wind picked up again once we were past the city limits, but for the first time since my father's birthday, it blew in our favor. Feeling its gentle push at my back, I said a silent thank-you to the cycling gods and brought my speed up to 20 mph with little effort.

Across the scenic farmlands, I spotted children playing in the shadow of a large barn. They were a good distance away from the road but close enough that I could hear their shouts and laughter. The boys wore dark dress clothes and chased one other while the girls looked on quietly. They wore full-length dresses made from simple material and plain bonnets tied beneath their chins with cloth strings. As we rode by, they stopped their games and stared in our direction.

Earlier that morning my father mentioned that our route would take us through Amish country. During my college days in Harrisonburg, Virginia, I'd often joined my fellow JMU Triathlon Club members on their weekly bike ride—a flat, ten-mile stretch a short distance from campus that took us through Amish country. The Amish always offered friendly waves from their fields and their front porches whenever we passed. More often than not, we'd encounter a horse-drawn buggy trundling along the road, and our long line of riders would respectfully move to the opposite side so we wouldn't spook the horse.

I'd hoped to see a buggy as the three of us continued to ride, but aside from the occasional car, there was little to no traffic. One smartly dressed Amish gentleman tipped his wide-brimmed hat as we pedaled by, and I waved, satisfied at the small connection with a stranger. The diversity of our country simply amazed me. Earlier in the day, I'd seen wealth beyond my imagination, and not two hours later, I was witnessing the simple lifestyle of the Amish.

By early afternoon, almost everyone had finished the ride to Tuscola. There was nothing left on the schedule until RAP that evening, so after settling into our motel room, I typed my latest blog entry, reflecting on the day's events. A few short weeks before, I would have considered seventy-seven miles on Shiva a heroic feat. But after riding her more than two thousand miles between Costa Mesa, California, and Tuscola, Illinois, seventy-seven miles seemed to be almost a day off. I was amazed at how much could be achieved with a simple change of perspective. Just as shifting the gears on a bike changes the resistance a rider faces on the road, shifting mental gears can change the resistance we face in life.

Small-Town American Pride

Day 23: Tuscola, Illinois-Lebanon, Indiana
Distance: 120 Miles
Total: 2,341 Miles

FOR MOST OF THE MORNING, WE ENJOYED GENTLE TAILWINDS PUSHING us along lightly trafficked country roads that crisscrossed maturing fields of corn and wheat. Around midday, we picked up Highway 150 in Danville, bid farewell to Illinois, and said hello to the ninth state of our ride, Indiana. We were now in Hoosier territory. Mike had jokingly explained that the term *Hoosier* harkened back to early French settlers because whenever a visitor came calling, they'd call out, "Whose there?" I later discovered the term actually comes from a poem written by John Finely, but I liked Mike's colorful explanation better.

As soon as we crossed the Indiana state line, I asked my father if we could finally adjust our watches to eastern standard time. When he gave me the go-ahead to gain an hour, I grinned like a Cheshire cat. I was back in the zone where I'd spent my entire life!

It soon became clear why Indiana is part of America's Corn Belt. We passed rows and rows of neatly arranged crops, and I tried to imagine what the state, with its organized fields stretching for miles, must look like from a bird's-eye view. We seemed to be riding through living postcards or a Norman Rockwell painting depicting small-town America. Farmers wearing battered John

Deere hats steered their tractors through hardy crops. At the edges of the fields sat small farmhouses, corn silos, and large red barns that could have been rendered with a painter's brush. The scent of freshly turned earth, along with the unmistakable smell of recently deposited manure, wafted through the air.

Spaced among the fields and the machinery were groves of tangled vegetation and gnarled trees known as windbreakers. I learned that during planting season, windbreakers keep newly sown seeds from being blown away by the breezes that constantly sweep across the flatlands. Each time we rode past one of the thick walls of vegetation, the sound of the wind died down and silence suddenly reigned. Sometimes when I hadn't seen one of the windbreakers coming up on the road, the abrupt cessation of noise caused me to look up sharply in confusion. The absence of the wind unnerved me. It had become such a constant companion during the past three weeks that at times I felt its presence just as strongly as my father's.

Compared with the endless days in the Midwest with harsh elements and relentless hills, the Indiana terrain was pure joy. I trailed lazily behind the two other Wolf Packers so I could soak in all the state had to offer. During RAP, Mike told us he was fond of Indiana. In his younger days before joining the air force, he had called it home. He spoke warmly of the hardworking, pleasant people and declared that the state possessed what he called "small-town charm." Small towns seemed to spring up every five to ten miles between the fields of gently swaying crops. At the entrance of each community was a large, colorful welcome sign on the side of the road. Each sign declared the same three things—the name of the town, its population (usually in the low triple digits), and a catchy phrase unique to that town. "Welcome to Hillsboro. The home of 600 happy people and a few old soreheads" topped the list of my favorite greetings!

A Main Street ran through the heart of each town with mom-and-pop shops hugging each side. Intersecting streets led to friendly-looking neighborhoods where in backyard after backyard laundry, snapping gently in the breeze, hung on clotheslines tied between trees. White picket fences enclosed manicured lawns where children played while mothers and older folks watched over them. American flags hung above front doors or were on display behind store windows, celebrating the upcoming Memorial Day holiday. Red-white-and-blue ribbons were tied around lampposts, and larger flags swayed from poles on street corners. In the carefully trimmed yards, "Support Our Troops" signs were planted firmly in the ground. It was a stirring sight to see so much patriotic pride on display and once again I felt blessed to see it all from the seat of a bicycle.

After our SAG lunch, we had no more than a couple of final turns to go before arriving in Lebanon. Because a few of the roads on our route were unmarked, several riders gained some bonus miles, but thankfully, I navigated right to the motel parking lot and for once I wasn't last. That night as I pulled the sheets under my chin, I looked at my watch glowing in the dark. It read 10:00 p.m. I thought of my friends and family back on the East Coast going to bed at the same time. I said good night to them all and fell fast asleep.

Making the Connection(s)

Day 24: Lebanon, Indiana–Richmond, Indiana
Distance: 107 Miles
Total: 2,448 Miles

My father and I had our latest start to the day since the ride began. Many of the riders had met in the lobby at a quarter till seven and had piled into two ABB vans for a field trip to Roark Fabrication. The local manufacturing company was mainly invested in aerospace technology but was also known for building custom titanium-alloy bicycles for serious cyclists. My father and I had decided to forgo the trip in favor of extra sleep, but apparently we were too used to rising before the sun, because despite our best intentions, we were both wide awake at seven thirty.

With extra time on his hands, my father decided to do gentle stretches and warm-ups to loosen his back. The past few days hadn't been terribly difficult, but he didn't want to chance being sidelined again. I busied myself checking our equipment and charging my laptop. When he finished stretching, we took the elevator downstairs for breakfast and found a few solitary riders seated among the mostly empty tables. It felt strange sitting down for our meal without the usual soft chatter in the room. Still, we enjoyed taking our time eating, and not long after we finished, the group returned and the usual bustling activity began as everyone hauled luggage and cycling gear across the parking lot toward the ABB trailer. My father handed our bags to Jim, and as I scrawled my signature next to my name, I kept an eye out for Joe so we could ride together. Soon everyone was clipped in and heading out.

By midmorning, the temperature had climbed ten degrees higher than it had been the previous day, so many riders sported short-sleeved jerseys and traded in long pants for cycling shorts. It was a welcome sight to see George whizzing past me in his trademark powder-blue outfit. My father opted to wear his official red ABB jersey, and I couldn't help but notice it fit much more loosely around his torso and his arms. Without the bulky layers of heavy clothing, it was clear he'd lost a significant amount of weight over the past few weeks. With all of the riding hours, it wasn't surprising that most of us would shed a few pounds, but my father seemed to be losing more than anyone else.

Barry frequently joked with us that one of the best things about these long-distance rides was the fact that he could eat whatever he wanted and not gain a single pound. My slow metabolism doesn't part with calories too easily, but for the first time in my life I could eat anything I desired and still lose weight. My father and brother have incredible energy levels with metabolisms to match, but I was a bit concerned about my dad as I watched him riding in front of me. He seemed to be literally shrinking before my eyes! Throughout the day, I kept asking him if he was feeling okay, but he just smiled at me with his usual positive attitude and replied with his trademark saying, "Another one in the books!"

By late afternoon the temperature had climbed past eighty degrees. The warm sunshine felt wonderful, and it seemed to bring people out of their homes and onto the lawns and the sidewalks. I was grateful to be out in the light, but couldn't help remembering a time when that wasn't the case at all. So many times when the days were nice and sunny, I'd close my blinds to block out the light. I preferred overcast skies and wet weather because in my depressed mind, a rainy day was the perfect excuse to remain motionless. On the weekends, I watched in silence from my window as students made their way up and down the sidewalks, loud, jubilant, and seemingly secure in their youth. The fears and doubts about my own life felt so far away from their happy college lives. In the evenings, they laughed and danced as I once did.

All of my life I had been certain of my place in the world with my morals firmly on point. But that was no longer true as I drew further away from the world outside and deeper into myself. I stayed in my room, which was not much larger than a walk-in closet, more and more. The days turned into weeks and then into months. One of the most terrifying things about this time was the sheer pace and ease with which I slipped out of view from family, friends, and teachers. There was no loud declaration. Instead, my unraveling came in a steady string of excuses, unanswered telephone calls, and increasingly meek apologies.

At first, drugs and alcohol were a source of comfort that helped block out the negative emotions that were beginning to pile up within me. They kept my increasing anxiety from overwhelming me completely. I built a wall out of these temporary distractions so that I could ignore the glaring fact that I had completely lost control over my direction in life. When I was sober enough to allow clearly formed thoughts to penetrate the haze, I would feel disgrace and shame at how far I had allowed myself to fall. Wake up. Smoke. Shower. Smoke. Maybe go to class. Try to get through it without falling asleep. Come home. Smoke and drink alone while mindlessly watching movies until I fell into a restless sleep.

In the end, I found myself completely alone in a prison my fear had created. I grew so afraid that even going out to buy groceries seemed like a painful ordeal. My world slowly shrank until it consisted only of my bedroom, my bathroom, and a short walk to the kitchen so I could feed myself once a day. Somewhere, in the far reaches of my confused mind, I knew if I stayed on the road I was traveling down, only bad things awaited me. I would fail out of college and possibly lose any chance of doing something worthwhile with my life.

One evening I looked at the four walls of my room with the horrible realization that this tiny space had become my entire world.

I didn't sleep more than an hour or two the whole night, because I knew I had reached a fork in the road and had to choose. Things would never be the same again if I picked up the phone and told my parents that I was drowning in sadness and needed help. But I also knew that breaking the silence paled in comparison with what might happen if I stayed alone in my room for one more day. As the sun came up and streamed into my small window, I saw the light. There was still time to set things right, but I couldn't do it alone. So I picked up my phone with my heart in my throat and called home.

And now, only two short years later, it hardly seemed possible that my world had gone from a room roughly four hundred square feet to the entire beautiful landscape of the United States. One of Mike's favorite sayings throughout the ride was "The more you see of the country, the bigger your own proverbial backyard will seem." With each man, woman, and child I passed, I gained a deeper understanding of what he meant. I thought about all the people I'd met since leaving the Pacific Ocean—countless shopkeepers, motel clerks, farmers, random citizens, and most of all, my fellow bike riders. They all had stories to tell, filled with challenges, uncertainties, triumphs, struggles, and joys. Every one of us is connected through these shared stories, and with each mile I pedaled, I realized that I deserved to make those connections and to share my life with the people I met. I deserved to live in their backyards, just as I welcomed them into mine. Never again would I live within shrinking walls of fear, guilt, shame, and addiction.

Eric Wagner was back in the world.

Old Friends and New Friends

Day 25: Richmond, Indiana-Marysville, Ohio
Distance: 106 Miles
Total: 2,554 Miles

THE NEXT MORNING, THE SUN SHONE ON ANOTHER PERFECT DAY FOR riding, and my father, Joe, and I felt the wind at our backs. Our mechanic Jim told me he called tailwinds like these—ones with a gentle but firm push—hero winds. I understood what he meant, because I was cruising at a speed that left me breathless from excitement, not exertion. I felt like some kind of Captain America cycling superhero with a cape billowing behind me as the pastures and the fields blurred together in streaks of color. It seemed as if the weather in the eastern portion of the country was trying to make up for the rough conditions in its western counterparts. Our whole ABB team still grimaced when we talked about Dalhart, Texas, but this day all we had to do was sit back and enjoy Mother Nature in her best mood. By midmorning, I happily yelled "Hello, Ohio!" as the Wolf Pack raced along, faster and faster, and crossed into the tenth state of the trip. Besides the weather, I had another reason for my happy mood. Someone special was waiting for my phone call later in the day so she could visit me in Marysville, and I couldn't wait to see her.

I was eleven years old when I first saw Noelle at Mount Olive Middle School, and we were fast friends from the day we met. Everyone naturally gravitated toward her kind and friendly personality. Noelle had a beautiful heart-shaped face, shiny brown hair, and an infectious smile. I couldn't count how many of my friends had a crush on her at one point or another. A gifted athlete, she was the only girl I'd ever known who played on an organized football team alongside the guys. She'd sidelined a few with broken bones, and I'm not ashamed to admit I felt the wrath of her tackles more than once. On and off the field, Noelle was respectful to coaches and teammates. In and out of the classroom, she was just as gracious to teachers.

When we were kids, Noelle told me she loved animals and wanted to be a veterinarian when she grew up. We still joke about the time she wanted to dissect a pet hamster after it died, because she was so curious about its organs and bones. I never doubted she would achieve her professional dream, and I was right. Noelle had used her athletic ability to gain a Division I scholarship for field hockey at the University of Delaware. After graduating from college, she moved to Ohio to attend veterinary school at The Ohio State University.

I wasn't sure where in Ohio Noelle lived or whether she would be close to our route, but I figured it couldn't hurt to let her know I was passing through the state. As it turned out, Noelle lived close to Marysville, and she said she'd be happy to come to the motel. I was excited about seeing her after so many months apart, though we'd stayed connected through my blog. Since the day we left Costa Mesa, she'd sent me uplifting messages, particularly after a hard day's ride. And after more than three weeks with baby boomers for company, I was thirsty for conversation with someone closer to my age.

With the help of the hero winds, the miles through Ohio flew by. A few hills rose up every now and again, making it necessary to drop gears, but compared with Missouri, this was nothing I couldn't handle, and soon we were all wheeling into the motel parking lot. I quickly guided Shiva through the lobby so I could take the elevator to our room and make a quick phone call to Noelle. Once I gave her the motel address, she told me she was only twenty minutes away, and we made plans to meet in a half-hour. I cleaned the mud and the grit off of Shiva until her silver sides gleamed. Glancing in the mirror, I decided I'd better do the same. It felt odd to be concerned about how I looked after so many days of not worrying about shaving or even about how I smelled. Although I made a valiant effort to clean myself up each day, I must admit that on some nights the bed called to me more loudly than the shower. Just as I was finishing up, my cell phone rang. It was Noelle!

I spotted her right away in the parking lot when she flashed me her big smile. My father was close behind me. He had watched Noelle grow up and was also looking forward to seeing her again. The three of us exchanged happy hellos and hugs and then headed into the lobby where several riders were milling around. As soon as I saw Joe, I brought Noelle over to meet him and proudly introduced the third member of the Wolf Pack. Joe smiled and told Noelle he'd heard all good things about her. Her smile grew wider, and she thanked him before saying she'd read good things about him, too. I beamed from ear to ear, watching one of my dearest friends talk with one of my newest. I spotted Mike and Barbara across the lobby, so I excused myself and walked over.

"Excuse me, Mike," I said. "I was wondering if you and Barbara could come over and say hello to my friend Noelle." Mike raised a questioning eyebrow. "She goes to veterinary school around here. She's heard a lot about the riders, and I'd really like you to meet her."

He and Barbara said they'd be delighted and followed me across the lobby. In our little semicircle, Mike told Noelle that he'd been working with ABB for some time and that we were a particularly tough group of guys. Noelle glanced at me as she said she wasn't at all surprised to hear that. I thanked Mike for the compliment and told everyone Noelle and I were going to grab a cup of coffee. As soon as we stepped back into the parking lot, we saw Barry posing for photographs with a large group of kids. A woman was busy snapping away as several other adults supervised. I asked Noelle if she wouldn't mind waiting a few minutes so I could introduce her to Barry. While we waited for them to finish, I explained this was his second time riding across the country to raise awareness of hemophilia and money for research. When the picture taking was finished, I asked Barry to join us after he helped the adults gather the children. "Like trying to herd cats!" he exclaimed before approaching us. He greeted Noelle warmly, and after we chatted for a few minutes, Noelle and I headed to a nearby coffee shop.

"So how has the ride been?" she asked, taking a sip of her iced coffee. I smiled faintly at the question, feeling the two sides of my personality waging war over how to respond. Part of me wanted to shamelessly brag about how amazing it all was. I wanted to toot my own horn so loudly that people in nearby states would know what a great cyclist I had become. The other part knew that as one of my oldest friends, Noelle wasn't someone I needed to wow with my story. "Hard," I finally admitted, "very hard. I know that some of my blog entries gave the impression that it's been tough, but that doesn't even come close to the real thing. In the first week I couldn't even tell you the number of times I had been certain that day was my last on the road."

"Yeah," she replied, "I know what you mean. Vet school is harder than anything I've ever gone through. I've never seen so many people in a classroom on the edge of a nervous breakdown. It's been an intense experience so far."

We chatted for a while until I reluctantly told her I had to get back to the motel for RAP. She said she had some studying to do before the next school day and needed to get going as well. Vowing to keep in touch, I wished her luck at vet school, and she wished me safe travels on the rest of the ride. After a last hug and a wave, I watched Noelle drive off. Though it had been for only a short time, some of the best influences of my life had joined together that day, and it had been wonderful to watch my old and new worlds meet.

Back in the motel lobby, my father told me our evening RAP was taking place in one of the meeting rooms on the first floor. As I walked in, several of the riders were setting up folding chairs in a neat circle, just like the circles for the Narcotics Anonymous meetings I'd attended while going through my substance abuse program. I remembered the first time I nervously walked in with my friend Simon, who came with me to every meeting for support. The chairs were the gray plastic kind that graced every banquet hall, church basement, and firehouse—the kind with flimsy screws that always wiggled under you as you sat down.

The room quickly filled with my teammates, and as Big Tom took his seat, he jokingly said, "Hello, I'm Tom and I'm a cycling addict." Laughter filled the room. I chuckled halfheartedly. *If only they all knew*, I thought, *what would they think of me?*

But even as the familiar harsh thoughts returned, I knew something had changed. The old memories didn't sting as much, and the demons that usually parked themselves in my sadness didn't stay very long at all. They simply had no place in this new circle. Peace and confidence were politely but firmly waging war against them. And this time they were winning.

Emotional Nutrition

Day 26: Marysville, Ohio-Wooster, Ohio
Distance: 103 Miles
Total: 2,657 Miles

CATCHING UP WITH NOELLE AND THE POSITIVE EXPERIENCE AT THE
RAP meeting left me feeling as if I could conquer the world, or
at least the United States, when I went to bed. During the night,
however, a dark cloud must have floated over the motel and landed
on me, because the moment my eyes opened, I saw the world in
muted shades of gray. My dad later would joke I'd gotten up "on
the wrong side of the saddle." The worst part was that for the life
of me I couldn't pinpoint what was wrong. All I knew was it took
every ounce of energy I had just to get out of bed and I had to cover
a hundred-plus miles, with the last thirty-five including some hefty
hills, as Mike had noted at RAP. How in the world was I going
to do that when getting from the bed to the bathroom felt like a
Herculean effort?

I slipped into my cycling clothes and finished my usual routine.
There had been a few mornings when it had taken me a little longer
to get into the zone. On those occasions, I had dug through my gear
for my iPod, hit my favorite playlist, and grooved my way into a
good mood. But as I brushed my teeth and packed my gear, I could
tell that wouldn't work this day. At breakfast I was even angry over
the powdered eggs and instant oatmeal I'd grown accustomed to

eating each day. I was hungry, but nothing seemed appealing as I picked at my food. I told myself that by the time we were all clipping into our pedals, I'd be back to my old self.

No such luck. Wearily pedaling behind my father, I couldn't even appreciate the blossoming spring unfolding around us. After a few miles, I realized my exhaustion was affecting more than just my aching legs and back. It was weighing heavily on my mind as well. In the early days of the ride, I did everything I could to stay positive, to look adversity in the eye, and not to flinch. Over the course of two thousand miles, I'd been stretched to my limits plenty of times. Still, I had done everything humanly possible to keep going.

Including singing.

I love to sing. Granted my singing sounds better on some days than on others, but everyone who knows me knows that has never dissuaded me. My mother even hung up a sign in my bathroom at home that says, "Sing Like No One Can Hear You," in honor of my fondness for belting out a tune at the top of my lungs while in the shower.

At least once a day on the road, I would sing. When the rigors of the journey began to press down on me, I'd burst into whatever tune was playing in my head. When you're staring down a road in the middle of nowhere with cattle skulls, tumbleweed, and silence all around, the sound of a voice, even if it's your own, can work wonders. I thought I was alone most of the time I was singing, but at the end of one ride, Jan told me he'd never met anyone who liked to sing as much as I did. So much for being alone!

The Beatles' "All You Need Is Love" stayed in my top-ten playlist out on the road. Another favorite was the Doobie Brothers' "Black Water," which brought back a great memory. When I was five or six years old, my mother taught me to ride a bike without training wheels. I kept falling over because I was pedaling either too fast or too slow, so she sang that song to me over and over to help me keep time with my cadence. I remember her singing and running back and forth beside me in the empty parking lot in front of my elementary school until finally she let go and I was riding all by myself! Who would have thought that someday I would ride my bicycle a whole lot farther than the parking lot in New Jersey?

But that morning in Ohio I could conjure no mental energy for singing. Not even the fair weather or the beautiful scenes of dew-drenched meadows and groves of birch trees could lift me up out of my funk. Instead, with each mile I grew more and more aware of how far we still had to go before we reached Amesbury, Massachusetts. That thought sapped all of my strength, and as the day dragged on, I found myself snapping harshly at things that normally wouldn't irritate me.

Not even my dad's usual upbeat attitude could dispel my gloom. In fact, I found myself thinking, *For once in your life, could you not be so freaking happy? Not everything is going great, for crying out loud!* But he stuck with me the whole day, even when it was obvious I was in no mood for company. A part of me wanted to find a patch of soft green grass under a tree and to fall asleep, maybe even dream about being in my own bed and not having to wake up at five o'clock and to ride more than one hundred miles to the next motel. I was grateful that my father didn't leave my cranky mood or me because had I been alone, that soft green grass might have won out.

When we finally arrived in Wooster, Ohio, I didn't have enough energy to crack a smile. Mike hadn't been kidding about those climbs the last few miles, and I was more than ready for the day to be over. Once we reached the motel, I stumbled behind my father like some weird spandex-clad zombie. I didn't speak a word to anyone as we got on the elevator and by the time we arrived at our room, I was hanging on to Shiva's sturdy black seat for support. As soon as my father opened the door, I pushed past him and flopped onto the bed in a heap. When we'd finished our eleven-and-a-half-hour day in Albuquerque, New Mexico, I'd been just as tired, but that weariness had been tempered with a wild exuberance because I'd pushed myself beyond the brink of exhaustion and had survived the day. But at this point, I just didn't care. I felt no hint of triumph, only sheer exhaustion. We must have gotten our luggage at some point, although I only recall pulling out my laptop and falling asleep within minutes with my headphones still plugged into my ears.

When I awoke a few hours later, I was alone, my laptop was warm in my lap, and the room was dark. Blinking several times, I winced as my eyes protested against an unplanned nap with my contact lenses still in place. As I fumbled for the bedside lamp, my fingers brushed against something that hadn't been on the table before I fell asleep. Curious, I sat up and flicked on the lamp. A large white foam box sat beside me along with a tall foam cup with a thick lid and a straw poking out invitingly. I realized I was ravenously hungry, and I flipped up the top of the container. I saw a flash of something green, pebbled, and juicy and crammed whatever it was into my mouth. A burst of sweet and sour juices told me it must have been a pickle. Crispy potato chips were heaped in a pile next to a huge turkey sandwich. When I picked up the cup, I noticed its contents were heavier and more solid than a typical soft drink. After taking a sip, I discovered to my delight that it was a chocolate milkshake! The sip turned into a few hardy gulps, and then I focused on my sandwich. With each delicious bite, I felt renewed strength flow into my limbs, lifting my physical and mental energy levels. By the time I wiped the crumbs from my T-shirt, I was on my way out of bed.

Chocolate shake in hand, I checked my watch and saw I still had time to make RAP if I hurried. My father had left a spare room key on the nightstand. I slid it into my pocket on the way to the elevator and finished my shake as I walked down the hall toward RAP. I felt like a new man. It's amazing what a good nap and a good meal can do for the spirit. It wasn't until later that evening, after yet another big meal, that I realized what had happened to me during the day. Because I'd wanted to spend time with Noelle the previous night, I'd eaten only a small dinner. Consequently, before I had even opened my eyes, my body was depleted of the precious energy it needed to rebuild my muscles. Breakfast had been minimal, and then because I was so grouchy and eager to finish the ride, I'd barely touched the SAG lunch and the snacks offered throughout the day.

My thoughts returned to what George had explained on the first day of the ride. He'd introduced the term *bonking*, the equivalent of a marathon runner hitting the proverbial wall. My body had done everything I'd demanded of it for the past three weeks. All it had asked in return was that I feed and hydrate it properly. I had completely bonked during the ride and had no one to blame but myself.

Even though I'd been miserable company all day, my father had stuck by me. After his generous gifts of emotional nutrition in the form of unflagging enthusiasm and encouragement, as well as physical nutrition with a simple milkshake and turkey sandwich, I realized once again how lucky I was to be on this journey with him.

T-Shirt Swap

Day 27: Wooster, Ohio–Warren, Ohio
Distance: 98 Miles
Total: 2,755 Miles

OVER THE PREVIOUS FEW DAYS, THE ROUTE SHEETS MIKE AND KAREN handed out after RAP had been growing longer and longer. The one my father and I received for the ride to Warren, Ohio, was the thickest by far. Each page contained dozens of street names, mileage, and turns, all typed in two long columns on the front and back of each page. Even though most of us had a GPS attached to our bikes, we were grateful for the paper directions because you never knew when a Garmin might lose power or, even worse, fall off the bike and break. Sometimes, after more than nine hours of following directions—with technology, on paper, or both—the roads merged in a hazy fog of numbers and words. I secured my directions over Shiva's handlebars using binder clips. We'd logged hundreds of miles in the past week, and the last thing I wanted was a few extra bonus miles.

As we left the parking lot, it looked as if Mike's favorable weather reports had finally run their course. The roads were shrouded in fog and the temperatures were cool, but the Wolf Pack was prepared with long-sleeved jackets to keep the mist at bay. Riding through the silvery fog with Shiva beneath me and my father and Joe by my side, I felt renewed strength. The cool air against my cheeks was invigorating, and my legs felt fresh and ready to carry me through whatever the day held in store. No more bonking for this guy!

But each day brought its own set of challenges, and this one was no exception. With every passing mile through Ohio, the roads grew more difficult to navigate. Thick groves of trees pressed in on us as tufts of grass and shrubbery fought their way through the crumbling piles of asphalt below us. It looked as if Mother Nature was fighting to reclaim the roads civilization had poured over her. Potholes were so deep and wide that we were forced to cross to the other side of the street to avoid them. It took every ounce of concentration I had to steer Shiva into the "best" parts of the road and I just hoped I'd chosen correctly. A few times I wondered what would happen if we fell into one of the deepest ones, but I quickly decided I didn't want to know the answer. By the time we reached our motel in Warren, I'd spent most of the day bouncing against Shiva's frame. I was downright surprised that the Wolf Pack had made it without any punctured tires or fractured rims—or bones.

After a quick shower, I headed down for an early RAP. Barbara had said we should give ourselves plenty of time for the ABB time-honored tradition of the T-shirt swap. Two days earlier, when she had reminded the group about it, a ripple of surprise had crossed the faces of some riders. Clearly, not everyone had remembered to bring a T-shirt, and I'm embarrassed to admit my father and I were members of that group.

No sooner had Barbara mentioned the swap than my father had my mother on the phone, explaining our somewhat desperate situation. "What kind of T-shirt do you think we should get?" my father asked me. I didn't hesitate for a second. "Get something with a wolf on it!" I exclaimed. Grinning, my father asked my mother to ship the shirts express mail to the motel where we'd be in two days. She said she was on the task and would let us know when the order had been placed and shipped.

My mother is no stranger to bailing out the Wagner men, and as always, she got the job done. The shirts were waiting for us at the front desk of the motel in Warren, Ohio, right on schedule. I brought the package up to the room and eagerly tore into the wrapping to uncover two large men's T-shirts, each sporting a beautiful, howling wolf. Way to go, Mom! They were perfect for the founding members of the Wolf Pack. I told my father that our shirts would be a hit because even though there were technically only four members (Joe, my father and I, and Barry, an honorary member), every ABB rider was part of the pack since we were all on this journey together. As we headed down to the parking lot, he said he couldn't agree more.

Once we gathered in a circle, Barbara explained the rules. After the bearer of a T-shirt briefly explained why he'd chosen that shirt, he could swap it for another group member's shirt or steal a shirt that already had been swapped. According to the rules, there could be no more than three steals before a shirt was off limits. Barbara took out a hat and told us she'd written numbers from one to twenty-two (sadly, we had lost one rider to a family emergency), one for each member of the group. When it was my turn, I reached into the hat and pulled out a crumpled piece of paper with the number seventeen scrawled across it. I would be one of the last to go and hoped that all of the cool shirts wouldn't already be taken.

The riders who'd forgotten about the swap seemed to have rallied quickly, with the exception of Big Dan. Before we started swapping, he told us we had two choices. We could let him keep whatever T-shirt he managed to grab hold of by the end of the swap or we could take one of the unwashed shirts he'd recently worn. This wasn't a hard choice for any of us to make!

The swap began and T-shirts started changing owners. When it was his turn, Roger, one of the fastest riders and a member of the Four Horsemen, admitted that minutes before we gathered he'd run across the street to a nearby Marshall's to buy a shirt. He sheepishly held up all he could find on such short notice—a sheer-looking woman's blouse. Everyone burst into laughter. I looked left and right, wondering if anyone would dare swap for the offering. Joe valiantly stepped forward and took one for the team. He even bent his head down low so Roger could hang the blouse over his neck, as if Joe were an Olympic athlete receiving his gold medal. What a sight!

As my number grew closer, I fingered the soft cloth of the wolf T-shirt behind my back and wondered who might pick it. When Joe's turn came, he held up a shirt that looked like something a die-hard Cleveland Browns fan might wear tailgating before a game. It was the color of dried mud with a huge Browns football helmet emblem stamped across one side—obviously another quick purchase.

So far, the swap had been lighthearted and funny. Then Floris stepped into the circle to present his T-shirt. When he held up the shirt and began speaking in his Dutch-accented English, all the joking ceased. "Several years ago," Floris said, "I suffered a very bad back injury while training on my bike. It was horribly painful, and for a while I couldn't even walk. My doctors told me that perhaps I should start preparing for the fact that I would never be able to ride again." He paused and looked down at his riding clothes and his lean, healthy body, as if to say, "Yeah, right!"

"It took a long time, but I kept working at my rehab to get my back stronger," he continued. "Eventually, very slowly, I started to ride again. A couple of years later, I participated in a charity ride for the Dutch Cancer Society. The goal of the ride was to climb Alpe d'Huez seven times in one day. That's 3,600 feet of altitude each climb. In my mind, I believed that climbing a mountain seven times couldn't be done by just one person, so I chose to be part of a relay team. Before the event, my goal was four climbs, thinking that was reasonable. But on the day of the event, I kept on riding and climbing—four times, five times. When exhaustion kicked in, I remembered the charity and the people we were all climbing for, and that, along with the audience and the other riders, inspired me to push past my self-perceived limits. I climbed that illustrious mountain seven times by myself. On that day, I learned that we set limits in our minds, not in our bodies. Once we lift our mental barriers, we can do amazing things. By the way, I climbed it eight times the next time around."

Floris continued holding up his shirt for the group's inspection. "I wore this shirt a lot during those long months," he explained. "It was a hard time in my life, and it always reminds me what kinds of amazing things we can do with our bodies if we just stop listening to what our minds tell us we cannot do." When he stepped back out of the circle, I knew I had to have that shirt. But I wasn't the only one moved by his story, and it wasn't long before the shirt was selected, stolen three times, and off the market. I was hugely disappointed, but I still wanted to let Floris know how much his words meant to me even though I didn't get his shirt.

When it was my turn, my father and I unveiled our wolf T-shirts to the rest of the guys at the same time. There was a rumble of good-natured laughter as everyone enjoyed our little tribute to the Wolf Pack. Joe seemed especially pleased with our choice, though it was difficult to take him seriously with that blouse still hanging around his neck. It was time for me to swap my shirt, and looking around at the remaining possibilities, I saw Dan's sweaty T-shirt had yet to be claimed. No surprise there. There were a few other shirts that would fit someone half my size.

Finally, my gaze fell on a light blue shirt that Tim was holding. Tim was a strong and consistent rider, and during long stretches of road all I could see of him was a flashing taillight blinking from the back of his bicycle seat. His blue T-shirt had a cool design of bicycle handlebars with a caption that read, "Life Behind Bars." I laughed at the clever play on words and thanked him as I swapped his T-shirt for mine. My dad, proving yet again his easy and positive attitude, swapped with Big Dan. In no time, the exchanges were over, and all the riders seemed happy with their new shirts. Heading off in search of dinner, I broke away from the group and caught up with Floris. I told him that his willingness to be so open and honest about his trials had inspired me and that I was sad I hadn't been able to steal away his T-shirt. My new friend from Amsterdam patted my shoulder.

"What's your address, Eric?" Floris asked. "I'll send you a jersey just like it and, even better, one that I actually wore while climbing Alpe d'Huez. It will give you magic legs." Several weeks after I returned home I received a large package with *Amsterdam* written on the return address. I still wear that jersey during times on the bike (or in my life) when I need those magic legs he promised. I realize now that the true magic was in the honest message he'd shared about overcoming obstacles, especially ones that seem overwhelming. Floris had no way of knowing about the obstacles I'd faced in the past few years, but somehow it felt as if he'd been talking right to me.

Welcome to Pennsylvania—Again!

Day 28: Warren, Ohio-Dunkirk, New York
Distance: 139 Miles
Total: 2,894 Miles

A FEW MINUTES AFTER THE T-SHIRT SWAP, MIKE HAD TAKEN PHILIPPE, my dad, and me aside. Because we were slower than the rest of the group, he recommended that we consider leaving earlier in the morning to get a jump on the next day's ride of 139 miles. "You have my permission to load your luggage first and head out before everyone else," he said, "because any way you cut it, tomorrow's going to be the longest day we've had on the road." I asked if Joe could leave early, too. By then, I considered us a package deal. Mike's stern, weathered face cracked into a smile. "Of course," he said. "We can't break up the Wolf Pack."

Though Mike's message sounded a bit grave, I knew he was, as always, thinking about our well-being. He had more experience on a bicycle than anyone I'd ever known, and his passion for helping others achieve their riding goals was evident in every decision he made. Whenever Mike rode with the Wolf Pack, he told us tales about past rides all over the United States. His baritone voice carried above the steady moan of the wind, easily transporting his listeners to wherever he set his stories. It seemed as if during the past fifteen years he had spent more time in the saddle than standing on his own two feet. He told us that from 1990 to the time we met him in 2013, he'd logged almost two hundred thousand miles on a bicycle.

Mike told us about the time a rider in front of him had carelessly stashed a windbreaker in the back pocket of his cycling jersey. When a strong gust of wind ripped the jacket free, it flew straight into Mike, wrapping itself tightly around his face. With his hearing muffled and his vision obscured, Mike had stayed carefully balanced in the saddle and had kept pedaling. Rather than lose his cool, fall, and possibly hurt the riders behind him, he had calmly reached up with both hands to free his face and had continued riding.

A few days after our intense ride into Dalhart, Texas, Mike told us about a time he'd fought through similar conditions. The winds had been so strong that day that the tall grass on either side of the road didn't sway. It was pinned to the ground! "On a day like that, your world shrinks until it consists of nothing more than the road inching in front of you and the unseen wind howling in your ears," he said. "Yet somehow you continue to move forward and finish the ride."

Heeding Mike's advice about the long day ahead, Joe, Philippe, my dad, and I woke up earlier than usual and met in the lobby before the sun rose. After a quick breakfast, we silently loaded our luggage into the empty ABB trailer parked in front of the motel. Jim wasn't there yet, so we pushed our luggage as far back into the trailer as possible and signed the clipboard. At this hour, the morning was so quiet that every sound seemed magnified. Even the pen scratched loudly against the paper.

Riding into the deserted streets, we traveled in a loose, informal line with Philippe in the lead, Joe following Philippe, my father close behind Joe, and I brought up the rear. Not long after the motel was behind us, my father announced to the group that his Garmin wasn't working. "Can't get the route of the day on the screen," he told us, keeping one gloved finger pressed firmly against the power button to no effect. "Joe, Eric, what do yours say?" His question hung in the air, unanswered for a long moment as Joe checked his device. "Mine isn't working, either," he sheepishly reported. "I forgot to charge it."

"Eric?" my father asked hopefully. I held my tongue for a few heartbeats before admitting that I hadn't brought mine. On the longest day of our ride, I'd left behind one of the most important tools for navigation that a modern-day cyclist could own. Needless to say it wasn't my proudest moment.

"Don't worry, friends!" Philippe cheerfully called back. "Mine is working." A long pause followed as we simultaneously realized the situation we faced. Three out of four of us had only the route sheets on our handlebars. Just one wrong turn while following those lengthy pages of directions and there could be a lot of unwanted bonus miles on the longest day of the ride. In the back of my mind, a warning signal began to flash. It wasn't that I disliked or didn't trust Philippe. He had a great sense of humor and loved adventure. But Philippe could also be a bit stubborn. On more than a few occasions over the past few weeks, the ABB staff had to remind him to hug the side of the road rather than to ride directly in the middle of it. At first, our friend from Israel would oblige, but without fail, he would sooner or later drift into traffic again.

Should we call our situation in to the support team and have Karen or Barbara swing around with the vans, I wondered, *or stick it out and trust in our single GPS?* There wasn't much time to ponder the situation, because Philippe was making a right turn at the first intersection a few feet ahead of us. And like lemmings heading over the cliffs, we followed.

As the minutes and the miles ticked by, I grew less and less certain of our course. I referred repeatedly to the directions secured to Shiva's handlebars. Each bulleted point on the columned list came with a street name, the exact distance to travel before each turn, and the direction of the turn. So far, nothing on my route sheet matched up with anything we'd passed. Finally, my father spoke up. "Philippe," he yelled out, "are you sure we took the right turn?"

"We're going the right way," Philippe confidently replied. "The GPS says so." Each time we asked Philippe if we were headed in the right direction, he grew more and more adamant that we weren't lost. At the end of our first hour, we came upon a large sign welcoming us to Pennsylvania. Checking the directions, I realized we'd reached the state line a good twenty miles before we were scheduled to do so.

That was the final straw. My father and Joe came to a skidding halt on their bikes and stopped beneath the sign. My father pulled out his cell phone and searched for the ABB number to call for assistance. I dismounted from Shiva and leaned her gently against the welcome sign as he tried to explain to Karen exactly where we had ended up. "We're on the Pennsylvania state line," he said feebly. "I'm not even sure what road we're on." We spent the next fifteen minutes trying to pinpoint our location until Mike got on the phone and told us to follow the road to the nearest gas station. I heard his southern accent from where I stood. "Call this number when you get there," he told my father. "Jim will guide you in the rest of the way."

The ride down the street was intensely quiet. By the time my dad had gotten off the phone, we learned we'd gone more than twenty miles off course within the first thirty-three miles. I could tell by the set of my father's jaw that he wasn't too happy about it. Philippe apologized for not listening sooner but remained set on following his GPS. We pleaded with him to stay with the group, but when we arrived at the gas station, he stopped only long enough to buy a few things before pressing on down the road by himself. I'm still not sure what possessed him to stick with his route, especially since there was no telling where it would take him.

Soon after Philippe was gone, we spotted the familiar ABB support van. After riding along unknown roads, it was a relief to see Jim's bemused face peering out from the driver's-side window. He slowed down to say, "There's a parking lot up ahead a few hundred feet, so keep riding and I'll pick you up there." As he helped load our bikes onto the roof rack, Jim explained that because we had fallen so far behind the rest of the group, we'd never be able to catch up unless he gave us a lift part of the way. Looking down the road, he asked us where Philippe was. We all exchanged looks but said nothing. Jim caught our expressions and didn't press the issue as he finished tightening the last strap on the bike rack.

I sat in the rear seat of the van and sprawled out on the wide, comfortable cushions. Resting my head against the back of the seat, I enjoyed the sensation of moving swiftly even as the van creaked and squeaked with every bump in the road. It took less than a half-hour for Jim to drive us the twenty miles to the correct route and to put us back on the road. Carefully stepping down from the van in my cycling cleats, I thanked him as he scrambled onto the roof to hand Shiva to me. Except for my dad and Joe, there were no other riders in sight. Jim said they were only a few miles ahead. "You'll be able to catch them," he confirmed. "No problem." I felt renewed energy once we were back on track, and I silently thanked every member of our support team for getting us out of a jam. I soon spotted another sign welcoming us to Pennsylvania and thought to myself, *That sign should say, "Welcome to Pennsylvania AGAIN, Eric, Joe, and Ralph!"*

We linked up with some of the other riders a few miles down the road. George greeted us with a few of his usual British quips and welcomed us back to the group. Apparently word had spread quickly up and down the road that the Wolf Pack had seriously run off course. Thankfully we didn't stay in Pennsylvania too long the second time around and soon entered our third state of the day, New York.

The morning cloud cover steadily dissipated, and the afternoon sun shone at last. The shoulder of the road grew wider and smoother, and I relaxed for the first time that day. Looking through a thin grove of trees, I glimpsed sparkling sunlight reflecting off of a large body of water. The moment the tree cover broke and I got my first good look, all the negative thoughts about the morning's adventure were quickly forgotten. We had reached the shores of Lake Erie! The great lake stretched as far as the eye could see before dipping below the horizon. Its sheer size made it look more like an ocean than a lake, and for the rest of the afternoon it remained our constant companion as we hugged its coast for miles and miles. Along the way, Joe pointed out a large vineyard on the right-hand side of the road that supplied grapes for Welch's Grape Juice.

We had only a few miles left to the motel when I noticed my

father's cadence slowing. He'd grown quiet, but when I had asked him if he was okay, he repeatedly told me he was fine. His face was drawn, and I could tell that each pedal stroke was bringing fresh discomfort to his back. Finally, he admitted it was tightening up again, so I slowed my pace to ride alongside him. I was trying my best to encourage him when George, who'd been riding in front, pulled back and asked us what was going on. When I told him my dad was having a hard time with his back, he told us a quick story that made us all laugh.

"I had a friend back home I used to ride with, a really nice fellow who fell off the bike one day and broke his collarbone," George said. "Instead of going to the emergency room like we wanted him to, he told us MTFU." He grinned and winked mischievously. "That night he went to a concert he had already bought tickets for and went to the hospital the next day." George rode ahead, leaving us with bewildered looks on our faces. MTFU? We pondered the acronym for a few miles and all came to the same conclusion at the same time. We laughed and exclaimed, "Man the @#$% Up!"

Once again, my father did exactly that. With grim determination, we pulled into the parking lot after riding more miles in one day than I ever thought humanly possible. Philippe didn't arrive at the motel until another hour had passed. When he walked his bike through the revolving doors, he told me that his Garmin had reported an extra four thousand feet of climbing and that he had ridden more bonus miles than I'm sure he cared to count.

Even the Tires Are Tired

Day 29: Dunkirk, New York-Batavia, New York
Distance: 87 Miles
Total: 2,981 Miles

PLENTY OF EVIDENCE PROVED THE RIDE WAS STRAINING BODIES, BIKES, and gear. More and more riders wrapped their joints and ligaments, and more and more bikes required the attention of our steadfast mechanic, Jim. Shiva and I had definitely joined both groups. Just a few miles after George's MTFU story, my right knee started aching but with only a few miles before day's end, I'd kept quiet about it and pushed forward. During dinner, though, the ache had steadily grown worse, radiating down into my calf and my shin. I approached Big Tom and asked him about the black tape he kept wrapped around his knees. "Does it work?" I asked uncertainly. "Does it stick to your legs even with all the sweat?"

Big Tom nodded with unusual seriousness. "It does the trick all right," he said. "Just follow the directions on the side of the box, and make sure you wrap it tight." He handed me a box with one roll left inside. "It will definitely stick the whole ride as long as you don't mind losing a few leg hairs when you peel it off." I took the box up to my room, read the directions, and decided that if my knee didn't feel better overnight, I would give the tape a try. In the morning my knee still felt tender and sore so I applied the tough, sticky fabric to my bare skin, trying not to think about

217

how painful it would be when I pulled it off. But at least it would stay put.

The list for mechanical services had been growing longer each evening after RAP. Everyone was still talking about the time when Big Dan's strong legs had completely broken his pedal off of the crankshaft of his bike. He had to be driven to a bike shop to replace it so that he could ride the next day. Shiva was starting to show signs of wear and tear too. Her gears were sticking when I shifted them too quickly. I would hear a steady clicking, followed by a split second of grinding until the gears finally caught. The electrical tape I had wrapped around her handlebars was thin and tattered and it would be only a matter of days before it unraveled completely. And speaking of unraveling, my gloves were literally falling apart at the seams. Holes had formed in the palms, and the fabric between my fingers had worn so thin I could feel each fresh gust of wind tickling my knuckles. Still we all kept pedaling.

My father, Joe, and I started the ride to Batavia, New York, with Lake Erie's coast on one side of the road and rows of vineyards on the other. During our first SAG stop, we were resupplying our snacks and drinks for the next thirty-five miles when we overheard talk among the riders that the group was suffering a serious number of flat tires. Some were due to steady leaks, while others were dangerous blowouts requiring immediate attention. A bicycle tire is made of tough outer rubber and an inner tube that keeps everything inflated. When one of our teammates, Norman, experienced a tough blowout, Mike reported there had been almost nothing between the inner tube and the outer rubber or between the outer rubber and the asphalt. Even the tires were tired.

Over dinner in Dunkirk, New York, our mechanic Jim had approached my father about his form in the saddle. As he spoke, he used his hands to demonstrate the motion he wanted my father to use. "With each downward pedal stroke, you want to bring your foot back like you are scraping gum off of your shoe," Jim explained. "You want to keep continual pressure on your pedals. That way you're always moving forward, even when you're bringing it back.

Since your cleats are locked in, you can apply pressure on both the forward and back stroke of each pedal rotation." Apparently, my father had been riding his bike incorrectly for twenty-five hundred miles!

Armed with this new knowledge, my dad was a new man on the bike the next day. The difference in his form was amazing as he sped along the streets of New York. "Another one in the books!" he yelled exuberantly, his legs pumping. I laughed breathlessly and raced to catch his fleeing form. Seeing him carefree and enjoying the road, rather than hunched over in silent discomfort, was a huge boost. We raced along straightaways, winding turns, steep hills, and steady declines. For company, we had nothing but fresh air, warm sunshine, and empty roads. My dad told me later that night he suspected that because of the incorrect way he had been riding, he had been working twice as hard as the rest of the riders. No wonder he'd been losing weight faster than anyone else!

The eighty-seven miles to Batavia went by in a flash, and I was anxious to get to the motel because Big Dan had vowed he'd tell me one of his famous jokes. It seemed I was always showing up right after he told one to the rest of the laughing riders, so I made him promise he'd tell me one before we hit the Atlantic Ocean. As we approached our last few miles to Batavia, I spotted Big Dan's hulking frame churning up the road several hundred yards ahead and Shane's smaller form riding steadily behind. I fed some speed into Shiva's pedals and quickly gained on the two of them. Big Dan was happy to see me, and together the three of us pedaled into the parking lot. Shane wheeled his bike into the lobby while Big Dan and I watched my father and Joe finish their day. The four of us lingered at the entrance to the motel, chatting about the ride.

I watched Big Dan with expectant eyes, but he seemed content to let me suffer until I finally begged him to tell me a joke. "C'mon, Dan," I pleaded. "Tell me the one about the leprechaun in the bar. Everyone else has heard it, and they all say it's one of the best!"

"Sorry, buddy. That one is too adult-themed to be told in public," he replied. "You never know who might be listening." He put one finger on his chin and thought hard, as if searching his memory banks for the perfect joke to tell. His face cracked wide open with a smile.

"So I have this buddy of mine who just went through a horrible divorce," he said. "Lost the house, the car, everything. He was going through a box of his ex-wife's stuff, and he pulls out this dusty old lamp. He's rubbing it to get some of the dust off, and poof!—out pops a genie." At the word *poof*, Big Dan threw his hands high and wide over his head. "The genie looks at my buddy and says that he can't grant him normal wishes, because his ex-wife is the true owner of the lamp. But, to make it fair, the genie decides that he can compromise and explains that whatever my buddy wishes for, his ex-wife will get double. My buddy says, 'Sure, why not?' and begins his wishes."

Big Dan held up one finger. "For the first wish," he said, "my buddy asked for a million dollars. As soon as the words left his mouth the genie looked at him and reminded him that his ex-wife would get two million dollars." Then Big Dan held up two fingers. "For his second wish, my buddy wished for a hundred-foot yacht. Once again, the genie tells him his ex-wife will get double, so her yacht will be two hundred feet. My buddy says, 'Sure, no problem.'" Big Dan held up three fingers as he looked at me and then at my father. "So for my buddy's last wish, he tells the genie, 'I want you to beat me *half* to death." As soon as he delivered the punch line, my body shook with laughter. I was still chuckling as we followed Big Dan through the lobby where a television was on in the corner of the room. When we saw the screen, our laughter immediately died in our throats.

Beneath pictures of complete destruction and catastrophic loss were the lines "Oklahoma City Tornado" and "Casualties Rising." Our team had ridden through the heartland just days before the tornado, and I shuddered to think how vulnerable we would have been had it dropped down on us when we had absolutely nowhere to hide. I was incredibly thankful we'd missed such dangerous weather, yet heartbroken for the people in its destructive path.

I recalled Mike Munk's words about my backyard growing bigger as we rode through the country. Oklahoma was no longer a distant spot on a map, a place I'd never concerned myself with. It was a real place, with real people who were suffering a loss I couldn't fathom. It was clear they'd lost homes, livelihoods, and worst of all, loved ones, all in a matter of minutes. They weren't just faces on a TV. This time, they were my backyard neighbors.

Help Is Not a Four-Letter Word

Day 30: Batavia, New York-Liverpool, New York
Distance: 122 Miles
Total: 3,103 Miles

NOBODY FELT MUCH LIKE TALKING THE NEXT MORNING. SADDLING UP after breakfast brought little relief from the sadness settling over our group. As we rode through Batavia, I tried to occupy my thoughts with the beautiful colonial houses on either side of the road, but they only served to remind me of my home back in New Jersey. Words couldn't express how lucky I felt that it would be standing there safe and sound when I returned.

I stared at my father and Joe quietly pedaling in front of me. By this time, their backs were such a familiar sight that I could probably pick them out a hundred yards away. Joe had loosened up, both on and off the road. When we met during our first breakfast in California, he'd been polite but tight-lipped. When I praised him for finishing his Ironman races, he had brushed me off with cool reservation. I wasn't even sure if Joe liked me at first, but when my dad had been sidelined after his trip to the emergency room, he had stuck with me all day. I didn't ask him to do that, because I'd been so intimidated by every rider that I didn't have the courage. But there he had been, quietly matching his pace with mine, as if helping a young, temporarily orphaned cycling novice was the most natural thing in the world to do.

And then a few days after that, when I chased him down after he took a wrong turn past the Sandia Mountains, I think he realized that I was with him for the long haul. Now a day didn't go by without lively conversations among members of the Wolf Pack and with any guests who happened to ride by. In these few short weeks, I had come to rely heavily on my father and Joe, as well as on Barry, Mike, Barbara, Karen, Jim, and all my companions on the road, to help me achieve an incredible goal. It's amazing how swiftly complete strangers pull together in the face of overwhelming odds.

My thoughts turned once again to the scenes on television during breakfast. Sprinkled throughout the images of shattered windows, uprooted trees, leveled houses, and strewn cars were videos of ordinary people performing extraordinary acts of bravery and kindness. Neighbors helped neighbors sort through belongings and locate beloved pets. EMS volunteers spent sleepless nights searching for victims trapped inside buildings. People from nearby towns opened their doors to shelter those who had lost their homes. Strangers, both nearby and from all over the world, donated clothes, shelter, money, or even blood. Anyone with a cell phone could donate ten dollars with a simple text. Help comes in many forms, and it's how we get through life when times are tough.

Now please know that I would never compare my experience in college to the devastation facing the good people in the Midwest in May 2013. They had lost everything they cherished, through no fault of their own, in the blink of an eye with no more warning than sirens blaring minutes beforehand. I link my situation with that horrific event because once again, as I watched the post-tornado footage, I understood that we all need help at some point in our lives, and more important, it's okay to accept it.

I knew that I needed to ask my parents for help during my junior year. But each time I called home, instead of telling the truth, I would fill my voice with as much false optimism as I could muster as I lied to my parents about all of the great things happening in my life. I told them how much I was accomplishing and how much I loved my courses. I wanted desperately to tell them what was really going on, but hearing my mother tell me she and my father loved me and were proud of me made it that much harder to admit to her or to anyone else that I was drowning. *How can I possibly feel this way,* I thought, *when on the surface I have everything I could want or need?* I had worked so hard to get into James Madison University, the only college I'd wanted to attend. I had amazing friends and a family that loved and supported me. I was well aware that many young men and women would have given anything to have the life I lived and I was determined to see my way out of the mess I'd created without anyone's help and with as little notice as possible.

Obviously, that didn't work.

I'll never forget that early Friday morning in March 2011 as I sat alone in my room with the phone in my hand for what seemed like hours. After several failed dialing attempts, I finally let the phone ring. I almost lost my nerve when I heard my mother's cheery "Good morning, sweetie. How's my boy?" But I knew I had come to a crucial crossroads. I tearfully told her the truth: I wasn't even close to fine. Through chokes and sobs I told her I'd completely lost my way, was using alcohol and marijuana almost daily, and couldn't take one more day of pretending to be okay. I finally admitted I needed help.

At that moment, my mother was more than five hours away in New Jersey. Her first words were "I'm on my way and we'll get through this as a family. Now where's Patrick? You have to go wake him up." She needed help to be sure I was safe until she could get to me, so she turned to the young man she had known since elementary school. I woke up Patrick, and as soon as he saw my face, he knew I was in trouble. While my mother spoke to him, I sobbed with relief, thinking that maybe things could finally start to change. Patrick never left my side that morning as I unburdened my pain and sorrow to him, apologizing over and over for letting him and everyone else down. He said he was relieved I'd finally decided to tell the truth and said he knew things would be better for me now that I was figuratively and literally "out of the dark."

Less than six hours later, my mother walked up to the little wooden deck in our backyard and, with tears in her eyes, hugged me and said, "I'm so glad you called me, Eric. It's very brave to admit when you need help. I know you don't believe it right now, but I am very proud of you." She hugged Patrick and said, "Thank you, Patrick. I knew without a doubt I could count on you."

That morning I felt anything but brave. I felt like a huge failure. But now, after riding Shiva more than three thousand miles across the United States, facing 35 mph winds, broiling triple- digit heat, nineteen-degree windchill temperatures, endless hills, steep mountains, and major highways with bellowing trucks, I know making that call *was* the bravest thing I have ever done. Asking for and accepting help that day may very well have saved my life.

As I pedaled my way to the motel in Liverpool, New York, I reflected on the months of hard work after that fateful March morning as family, friends, teachers, and even strangers formed a tight circle around me while I pieced my life back together. In many ways, I'll never be the same Eric. I don't want to be because I know I've changed for the better. I'm wiser, more understanding, and extremely humble. I don't see or judge people the same way because I realize you never know what's going on inside them.

After dinner my thoughts kept turning to the people in Oklahoma and Kansas. I was grateful they had loving people surrounding them to help keep them safe for the moment and then help them rebuild their lives when the time came. And then I started thinking that maybe I could help others in my own way. Maybe my story would resonate with someone, somewhere, silently struggling alone in his or her own dark room. I wasn't sure how I would start, but I had a feeling that in time, my questions would be answered.

Confidence on the Road

Day 31: Liverpool, New York–Amsterdam, New York
Distance: 118 Miles
Total: 3,221 Miles

DURING BREAKFAST, MIKE HAD WARNED US THERE WAS A CHANCE FOR scattered storms throughout the day. There was little wind on the road, and the air felt thick and soupy with humidity that lay heavily on my skin. A line of sweat ran down my back, and the light fabric of the cycling jersey beneath my rain jacket was soaked through. I was wishing for just a little breath of fresh air to cool us when my eye caught a sign on the highway. It looked like any of the other hundred signs I had passed showing the upcoming cities and the mileage, but this one made my heart leap. Written across its green metallic surface in white letters was the town: Syracuse, New York. I knew that town!

I paused in mid-pedal stroke with breathless excitement as I waited for my father to reach me. "Is Syracuse University close to here?" I asked. "Yeah, not too far," he confirmed. "I had them in my March Madness bracket. Too bad they got knocked out so early in the tournament this year." He thought my question was somehow related to basketball, but I was just excited to recognize a town so close to home.

We quickly reached the crowded college town. Cars and trucks of every variety packed the streets. Motorists honked at each other, trucks rumbled past me, and I wrinkled my nose as we breathed in exhaust fumes. A few short weeks ago, riding these busy streets would have made me jittery. But instead of the usual tightness in my chest whenever things got uncertain on the road, I pedaled alongside Joe and my father with a cool confidence that had been steadily growing since the ABB group had left Springfield, Illinois.

Even being on a college campus felt different. I remembered my sadness when I rode through Northern Arizona State University in Flagstaff. Seeing all of the students with backpacks and smiles had brought back memories that I hadn't been ready to deal with yet, and I couldn't get off the campus fast enough. This time, however, all of those happy faces heading to class brought only well wishes from my now-quiet mind.

We left Syracuse and the flood of traffic slowed back to a trickle. Soon we returned to the quiet of the countryside, and to my delight, the Erie Canal greeted us. It threaded its way beside us to the right, sparkling brightly in the sun. This part of New York had seen heavy rain recently, and the grass and the trees on either side looked especially lush and vibrant. Toward midafternoon, Joe, my dad, and I linked up with two other ABB riders. It had been awhile since I'd seen Norman and Jody. Wordlessly, we settled into a pace line as they tightened ranks in front of and in back of me.

The last time I'd ridden in a pace line had been during that fateful day riding to Dalhart, Texas. Now that I was locked in, I wasn't sure how things would go, and I braced myself. But once again, something felt different. The burning self-consciousness and the negative running dialogue in my head, questioning every aspect of my ability to ride, was gone. Riding steadily along in my spot in the line, I was excited rather than afraid to be part of the group. The men riding with me were no longer the intimidating veterans of the road I'd met in California. They were my friends and I had earned the right to ride with them.

Mike had told us about a challenging stretch of road running through one of the small towns along our route to Amsterdam. Apparently, there was a steep drop-off on the shoulder. "Attention to details is important," he told us. "With only a few days left before the end, I want us all to stay alert. We're not out of the woods yet." Sure enough, the bumpy road came up quickly, yet I maintained my composure as our pace line continued into the town. Traffic was in full force, so I kept alternating my gaze between the flow of vehicles and the dangerous shoulder. Even with all the commotion, I heard the riders in front calling to those of us in the back, "Slowing! Slowing!" Half a dozen voices easily carried above the steady thrum of traffic. Gently, I squeezed Shiva's brakes and felt the familiar pull of her momentum. After so many hours in the saddle, she and I seemed to have merged into one entity.

The difficult road was soon behind us, and our pace line resumed its fierce progress. The miles dropped off, and by the time we pulled into the parking lot at our Amsterdam motel, despite gray clouds overhead threatening rain, I was on top of the world.

Keeping the Faith

Day 32: Amsterdam, New York-Keene, New Hampshire
Distance: 122 Miles
Total: 3,343 Miles

A BOOMING CLAP OF THUNDER THAT SHOOK THE FOUNDATION OF OUR motel jolted me awake in the middle of the night. At first, my sleep-muddled brain was convinced that I was a freshman back at JMU and that the train that passed through campus was making another late-night run. But when a blinding flash of lightning followed a few seconds later, I realized where I was and jumped out of bed to pull back the curtains. Heavy sheets of rain lashed at the windows as lightning flashed across the dark sky. As the storm's fury grew, the intervals between lightning and thunder grew closer and closer until they seemed to blur together in a single canopy of noise and light. Apparently, my father wasn't too concerned, because he slept right through the whole thing.

Cowering beneath my covers, I remembered what Mike had said at RAP while gathering us together in our usual huddle. He sternly warned us to keep a watchful eye on the sky because thunderstorms were appearing on the radar all along the route from Amsterdam to Keene. "Remember the rules of the road when you're hit with foul weather. When there's lightning in the sky, the first thing you do is find shelter because the last thing you want is to be exposed on your metal bike." He put special emphasis on the word *metal*.

Luckily, the storm had passed by morning, but the skies remained a dark leaden color and the air was damp. We hadn't pedaled more than one mile when we were confronted with some of the largest hills we'd seen since Missouri. It usually took about a half-hour for my legs to loosen up in the saddle, but the hills wouldn't allow such a leisurely adjustment period. The Wolf Pack was forced to claw and scrape up steep, wet roads on stiff, cold legs. My pulse spiked as beads of sweat dripped down my forehead. My wet-weather gear didn't leave much room for ventilation, and it didn't take long for the material to grow sticky against my skin.

The previous night's downpour had flooded the rivers and the creeks along the road, and they raged downstream in swollen sprays of white, foamy water. After a few hours of serious climbing, shafts of golden light pierced the clouds and settled in small gilded pools on the blacktop beneath our wheels. The terrain slowly flattened out, and I felt a shiver of relief as we finally said good-bye to the hills of New York.

My relief was short-lived as we said hello to our second state of the day, Vermont. It didn't take long for me to realize why Vermont is called the Green Mountain State. More steep hills lurked around every bend, and flanks of even taller hills pressed tightly against the narrow shoulder of the road, making me feel small in Shiva's saddle. New York had felt orderly and civilized with its neat roads and vineyards, but Vermont possessed a wilder, more untamed vibe. Brilliant colors shone through the fine mist coming from the streams, making tiny rainbows all around us. They offered a welcome diversion as we crept up the side of our first green mountain. "Are we having fun yet?" Joe called out from time to time. His question was met with grunts and a few colorful gestures, all in good fun, of course.

All that climbing quickly used up my breakfast calories, and I could feel my energy level dropping. After bonking as hard as I had in Ohio, I knew I'd never let myself experience that feeling again, so I asked my father and Joe if we could stop for a quick bite to eat before our first SAG stop of the day. Miraculously, the rain had held off, and I thought it would be okay to take a few minutes to sample some tasty Vermont food. I had been to Burlington many times to visit my older brother, where delicious farm-to-table cuisine lived up to its reputation. I promised my fellow Wolf Pack members it would be well worth the stop. Since none of us wanted to sit down in a restaurant with our damp spandex cycling gear, we kept a lookout for an establishment that could serve us quickly. A line of food trucks soon appeared on a bustling side street, and one of them boasted "the best local grass-fed burgers in town." We had found our spot!

The three of us leaned our bikes against parking meters and ordered quarter-pound cheeseburgers with all the fixings. The smell of the meat cooking made my mouth water. When the burgers were ready, we brought our plates over to a crowded picnic table and sat down next to some local residents. I don't think I had even touched the wooden bench when half the burger was in my mouth. A few folks gave me questionable glances, but I didn't care. The burger tasted incredible! It was juicy, hot, and bursting with flavor. I tasted the freshly squeezed ketchup, the melted cheese, the toasted bun, the crisp lettuce, the ripe tomato, and the grilled meat with every dripping bite. Wordlessly, my father handed me a few napkins to wipe the grease running down my chin. Although I nodded my thanks, I wasn't overly concerned about my appearance.

I was contemplating ordering a second burger when we heard the distant but distinct rumble of thunder. My dad, Joe, and I quickly finished up, threw out our trash, and with an extra spring in our steps, got back onto our bikes. The moment we turned out of the town, we began laboring up what appeared to be the steepest climb of the day. The entire quarter-pound of beef sat in my gut and with each additional foot of climbing, grew heavier and heavier. My scrumptious cheeseburger began turning against me, and my stomach painfully contracted with each breath. I was fairly certain that both it and I were going to end up on the side of the road. I was pedaling so slowly that I lost sight of Joe ahead of me. My dad must have been feeling even worse than I was, because he trailed farther and farther behind us.

Alone on the road, I decided the best way to make it up the steep climb was to put my head down and to take it one mile at a time. Whenever I dared risk a glance up the mountain, it looked like I hadn't even made a dent. By the time I made it to the SAG stop near the top, my legs were trembling and my gut was on fire. I could barely hold myself upright as I unclipped my shoes and dumped myself in a boneless heap into a nearby camping chair. *Whose bright idea had it been to order those cheeseburgers?* I wondered.

Only Joe, George, and Barbara were left at the SAG stop. When I told George that I didn't think cheeseburgers and mountains mixed very well, he simply shook his head and burst into laughter. I managed a weak smile as I waited for my dad to appear. As the minutes ticked by and he didn't show up, I worried that maybe his cheeseburger had indeed made a second appearance.

When I finally spotted my father at the foot of the gravel parking lot, I could tell that his stomach wasn't the only thing giving him a hard time. As soon as he saw me he barked out, "Tire's going flat. I could feel it deflating the whole way up … that!" He waved one gloved hand behind him to encompass the mountain we'd just climbed. His bike wobbled precariously as he dismounted to show us his rear wheel was more than half deflated. He'd made it up that mountain on not much more than rims and spokes. Luckily, Barbara was immediately on the case with her trusty bike pump and a spare tube from the ABB support van. My father's face relaxed with relief as he realized the rest of his day would be spent on an inflated tire.

We spent another fifteen minutes recuperating from the harrowing climb (and the cheeseburgers) before the Wolf Pack saddled up again. Our route took us through more rolling hills, each one greener and more lush than the last. My stomach finally started feeling normal again, and I powered my way to the peak of the next mountain. A sign declaring "Scenic View" enticed us, so we stopped to take a few photographs. The valley was spread out beneath us, and the forest felt peaceful and serene. I looked at my father and knew he was thinking the same thing I was: our majestic views of the country were quickly coming to an end. After a few moments, he nodded toward the storm clouds gathering behind us with silent strength. It was time to get going.

We immediately began a wild descent down the mountain. I'd grown accustomed to high speeds after hard climbs, but this was something else entirely. Shiva's tires hummed as they spun faster and faster against the wet pavement. Droplets of water sprayed up from her front tire, and soon my face was dripping wet. The trees around me turned into a solid wall of green, and the only thing I could hear was the rush of the wind past my ears. Fortunately the shoulders were wide and the streets empty and well paved. By the time the descent was over, we'd been speeding downhill for almost an hour. *That's the closest I'll ever get to flying without wings,* I thought.

Toward the end of the afternoon, we entered our third and last state of the day, New Hampshire. Despite constant storm clouds, the rain held off and I whispered a secret plea to our cycling gods, "Just a few more hours, please!" Several miles down the road, we linked up with Barry and then with George. Someone recalled that in addition to Mike's advice about the severe weather, he'd mentioned we'd be passing near an awesome milkshake stand. My earlier mishap with the cheeseburger had long been forgotten, and I wasn't about to pass up the opportunity for one last milkshake with my friends. I spotted a small roadside stand with a long line snaking its way from the ordering window. I guided Shiva through several picnic tables covered in checkered tablecloths and leaned her against a bench. While I waited in line, I caught the scent of french fries, and my empty stomach began making noise again. Just a few hours earlier it had been completely full; now it growled hungrily. It was just another day in the life of a cross-country cyclist and his "see food" diet. If he sees food, he eats it!

When it was my turn at the window, I ordered an extra large milkshake, french fries, and another hamburger. My father and Joe shook their heads and smiled. George finished his milkshake and took off down the road while Barry, Joe, my father, and I lingered. This was the last time the Wolf Pack would sit down together, and we wanted the fellowship to last a few more minutes. I looked at each weathered, sunburned face and remembered the day in Costa Mesa when the four of us had ridden together for the first time. There was no way I could have known then how much these men would come to mean to me. I felt closer to Joe and Barry than I could ever express in words, and the bond with my father had grown deeper and more meaningful with each mile we shared. I felt incredibly blessed.

And speaking of being blessed, as we were cleaning off the picnic table a dusty red station wagon pulled into the parking lot, and two nuns dressed in crisp black-and-white habits emerged. The driver, a woman dressed in civilian clothes, got out with them, and together they walked toward the milkshake stand. I must have been staring, because one of the nuns smiled in my direction. I had never seen a nun in person, much less talked to one, but before I knew it, I was walking right up to them. "Good afternoon, ladies," I said. "How is everyone doing?" They smiled at me and said they were fine. The woman dressed in civilian clothes explained there was a convent nearby. Apparently, nuns have a sweet tooth too, because like us, they were there for the famous milkshakes.

When they inquired about my cycling attire, I told them I was riding my bicycle across the country with my father. They thought that was a wonderful endeavor and wished us all the best of luck. In spite of myself, I asked them for their blessing and for a photograph for my blog. Who knew when I'd have another chance for a photo op with nuns? Without a second's hesitation, they agreed and we stood together for a quick photograph. I thanked them, and as we said good-bye, one of the nuns gave me her card. It was not a usual business card but a small card with a short prayer written on one side and a drawing of Mother Mary on the other. "Good luck, young man," she said, her warm eyes crinkling at the sides as she smiled. "Safe travels and God bless."

When we got back on the bikes, my head was whirling. The Eric who had started this trip a few weeks earlier had been jumping at his own shadow and wringing his hands nervously at the prospect of meeting strangers. Now I'd approached three women, two of them nuns, without so much as a second thought. I'd had no fear and no worry about being judged if I stammered or tripped over my greeting. That encounter with the nuns became one of the most poignant symbols of the ride for me. This was the Eric I had once known and I had the photograph to prove it! Instead of fear, I now had faith.

Not even the skies opening up with a torrential downpour dampened my spirits, though they sure did dampen everything else. With ten miles left to our motel, the thunder and lightning finally caught up with us, and we had nowhere to hide except under a grove of evergreen trees. As we huddled together, my father called the support van and, as if on emergency standby, Jim appeared within minutes. Silently, we loaded our bikes in the steady rain and piled into the van. The temperature had dropped sharply, and I shivered in my wet clothes, tucking my hands in my armpits for warmth. But by the time we reached the motel, the rain had stopped. Streaks of blue with a few rays of sunshine peeked through the clouds, seeming to prove what I had been thinking all day. Even after the worst of storms, the sun will always appear.

As I entered the motel lobby, my only thoughts were of a hot shower when a woman wearing a medical mask approached me, asking if I had seen Tom. I wondered whether she was sick or trying to avoid germs. Her kind eyes looked imploringly into mine from above the white material as I contemplated the question. There were two Toms on this trip. I'd seen Big Tom earlier, so I wearily replied, "I think he's around here somewhere." The woman thanked me and joined a man and a woman seated on couches in the lobby.

It wasn't until I was halfway down the long hallway that I remembered a conversation Big Tom and I had shared in Albuquerque. He told me he was raising money for a woman named Heather who suffered from a rare disease known as aplastic anemia, the failure of bone marrow to produce three types of blood cells— red, white, and platelets. Heather needed a costly bone marrow transplant, so Big Tom was raising money to help with her expenses. Her mask now made sense, and I kicked myself for not being more helpful. I hoped I'd see her again to properly introduce myself and to wish her well, but as usual, I barely had time to put Shiva in my room before reporting to RAP.

While Jim had been unloading our bikes, he told us that our last RAP meeting would take place in Mike's motel room. "Barry won't be able to make it to the banquet tomorrow night," Jim had said, "so he's going to say a few words tonight." My father and I made it to Mike's room with seconds to spare. Our last RAP went by quickly and efficiently as Mike told us where to meet and what to expect on the last day of our journey. After we rode onto the beach in Amesbury, Massachusetts, there would be a celebratory dipping of our front tires in the Atlantic Ocean. Later that evening, we would say our good-byes at a banquet with our families and our friends. But tonight, he said, it was Barry's turn.

Barry stood in the middle of Mike's crowded room and apologized for not being able to attend the banquet festivities. He was expected at another event, he explained, to celebrate his second cross-country achievement. Barry spoke quietly and sincerely about his life and the lessons he had learned living with hemophilia and HIV. "At one point or another we're all going to be sitting across from the guy in the white coat telling us something we don't want to hear," he said. "It's so important that we don't just live for ourselves but to help others when they're down. You just never know when it's going to be your turn."

By the time he finished, many hardened riders in our group had tears in their eyes, including me. I waited near the back of the room as everyone said good-bye to Barry. When it was my turn, I thanked him for helping me through the ride. I told him it had been a pleasure sharing the road with him and how much his story meant to me. The words seemed inadequate given how much he had helped me. "I'm sure I'll see you around, brother," Barry said after an affectionate smile and a firm handshake. "Keep on riding." Though we'd be sharing the road again for our final ride the next day, it was my first official farewell of the journey. The next day there would be many more.

Every Journey Has an End ...or Does It?

Day 33: Keene, New Hampshire-Amesbury, Massachusetts
Distance: 112 Miles
Total: 3,455 Miles

THE MOMENT I OPENED MY EYES I KNEW IT WOULD BE A DAY FILLED WITH all kinds of emotions. As my father and I got ready for our last day on the road together, I felt a mixture of ecstatic joy and terrible sadness. On the one hand, there would be no more rising at the crack of dawn to ride Shiva, no more cramped legs, no more aching back, no more dehydration, no more searching for calories to fuel my body, no more endless hills to climb, no more howling winds, no more bonking, and—dare I say it?—no more butt paste. On the other hand, there would be no more Wolf Pack, no more proving I had what it took to conquer another mountain, no more ABB staff helping at every turn, no more riders making me feel I was part of an amazing team, no more dinners together, no more SAG stops with Barbara smiling and reminding me to wash my hands, no more scenic views, no more meeting new people in every town, and no more days spent with my father by my side.

The motel room looked like every other room I'd slept in for the past four weeks and I was going to have a hard time walking Shiva out of the door for the last time. My father saw the look on my face and gently asked, "Ready to go?" I nodded wordlessly as we grabbed our bags and our bikes. My hand was wrapped tightly around Shiva's handlebars. She was looking ragged, with long streams of black electrical tape hanging down, but I loved her more than I could say.

As we ate breakfast, my mind rehearsed the day's events. We'd all meet at a crab shack three miles from our final destination. From there, we'd ride together in a group to the Atlantic Ocean where we'd ceremoniously dip our front tires into the water in front of family and friends waiting at the beach to welcome us back. More than a month had passed since we'd seen my mother, and I wondered how she would react to our physical transformations, especially my father's drastic weight loss. My older brother Matthew had taken time from his busy restaurant schedule to make the trip from Vermont to join us. He had been sending me encouraging messages throughout the trip, and I was looking forward to having the whole Wagner family together again.

For the last time, we all loaded our luggage into the blue trailer and signed in. The clouds from the day before lingered above us with the threat of more rain, and the storm had brought brisk temperatures. I pulled my rain gear over my extra layers for warmth and protection. A light rain started and quickly turned into a downpour as water dripped down the back of my helmet. But after all we'd been through, I thought, *What the heck is a little rain?*

After a few hours my stomach as usual demanded more food, and when I spotted a small grocery store I hastily guided Shiva underneath an awning, parked her next to a pole, and walked in. I selected a few items and brought them to the cashier. When she gave me my total, I felt around in my pockets before realizing my father had all of my money in his saddlebag. My cheeks burned with embarrassment and I muttered an apology to the clerk. Then out of nowhere, Philippe appeared by my side. He set his snacks down next to mine and told the clerk, "We are together." When I told him that I didn't really need anything, he gave me a stern sidelong glance, followed by a quick wink. My protest died on my lips. "Thank you so much, Philippe," I managed to say as I slipped the energy bars and the sausage breakfast sandwich into the back pouch of my cycling jersey. He didn't reply but the smile on his face grew wider.

Those words—"We are together"—meant so much more to me than the snacks. The two of us pedaled out onto the rain-swept roads. With the rain coming down even harder, my jacket became saturated and my feet felt as if they were freezing into blocks of ice. After a few miles our mechanic Jim rode up beside us. He continually called out to remind Philippe to hug the shoulder. "He's coming on our next ride," Jim told me, rolling his eyes. "I don't know what we're going to do with him!" Though Jim sounded exasperated, I knew he wasn't serious. Philippe could sometimes be absentminded on the road, but he'd never given up and we all admired him for his perseverance and spirit.

Eventually, the rain lightened back to a drizzle though the air remained cool. The chill had seeped into my bones, so I was pleasantly surprised when our SAG lunch was moved out of the elements into the lobby of a nearby motel. Once inside I was even more surprised to see Heather in full cycling gear standing next to Big Tom. She told us she was planning to ride with the group for a few miles. "Not too far," she said, her cheerful voice muffled behind her white medical mask. "I'll leave the long-distance stuff to you crazy guys!" Considering her frail condition and the foul weather, I was more than impressed that she wanted to ride.

I told Heather it was great to properly meet her and wished her the best of luck with everything. Her husband and a friend were there as well, and when I commented to the three of them that the weather was pretty nasty, her husband told me not to worry. "I'm like her own personal SAG stop," he joked. Behind his laughter, though, I could see his resolve to do whatever it took to keep his wife safe from harm. Heather's presence buoyed my waterlogged spirits, and as we parted ways, I said a prayer that she would win her struggle against the illness that threatened her life. Once again, someone else's journey made mine seem like a walk in the park.

About an hour before meeting up with the group at the crab shack, my father, Joe, and I linked up with Barry. I felt one final wave of nostalgia as the Wolf Pack pedaled the last leg of the journey together to our meeting spot. With each passing mile, the air took on a brinier quality. The soil grew lighter, and eventually little piles of white sand were visible under tufts of hardy grass. This could mean only one thing: the beach was getting close! Soon we were surrounded on either side by coastal waters. The sea was a dark, steely gray beneath an identical sky, but thankfully the rain had stopped. I was happy Mother Nature had decided not to soak us as we reached our final destination.

A big cheer went up as the Wolf Pack for the last time brought up the rear and rode into the parking lot of the crab shack. Red jerseys surrounded the four of us as all the other riders congratulated us. As I shook extended hands and slapped high-fives, I was overwhelmed by the finality of the moment. I'd envisioned it for so long that I could hardly believe it was happening. After several minutes, Mike hustled us into formation for photographs. The air was filled with clicks and bright flashes of light as the moment was immortalized. Outwardly, I grinned. Inwardly, I was in disbelief. After the photos were taken and each rider retrieved his camera or phone, it was time to ride the last three miles of our journey to join our families and our friends. In a sea of red, we rode en masse out of the parking lot.

I heard the beach before I saw it. Waves crashed onto the sand as seagulls called out. Above the familiar sounds rose the sharp wail of bagpipes. Colorful balloons soon came into view along with brightly painted banners and signs. The man playing the bagpipes was in full Scottish attire, complete with a knee-length kilt. Dozens of people were waving and cheering, and one look at a woman holding the Irish flag told me Shane's family had ventured across the ocean to welcome him back.

Amid the throng, I saw my mother and my brother running toward my father and me. My mother was smiling and crying. My brother, grinning from ear to ear, made it to us first and enveloped me in a huge hug. "Congrats, dude!" he said. "You did it!" Returning his hug, I turned to see my mom wide-eyed at my father's chiseled face. "Ralph!" she exclaimed. "You look so different. You lost so much weight!" She threw her arms around him and then pulled me close. "My boys are back! My tired boys are back!" The Wagner family stood, arms around each other, for a long time.

My father's eyes welled with tears at the magnitude of the moment. He said that accomplishing a lifelong dream with his son by his side would be a memory he would cherish for the rest of his life. That we were all together as a family to celebrate made the moment perfect.

Just as we began walking toward the dunes, a very tall gentleman appeared. "Bruce!" my father called out before he hugged him. One of his best friends from childhood had driven down from Maine for the special day. Bruce also was an avid cyclist, and it meant the world to my father that he made the trip. Together, we followed everyone onto the beach where Mike guided his riders to the edge of the ocean and lined us up. Side by side, we listened as he thanked families and friends for their support in his familiar southern drawl. Mike then turned to the men he'd kept safe for thirty-three days and thanked us for being a wonderful group of cyclists. At his signal, we all turned our bikes around and dipped our front tires into the Atlantic Ocean as a huge cheer went up from the beach.

The crowd grew quiet again as Mike reached into a bag and held up a battered water bottle. "We have a very special bottle of ocean water we've been carrying all the way across the United States," he said. "It's a little science experiment we're conducting to see if we can drain the Pacific Ocean one bottle at a time. We always choose one special rider to empty it out, and on this ride, we have two. The honor of pouring the Pacific Ocean into the Atlantic Ocean goes to two very, very tough individuals. They weren't the fastest cyclists in the group by any means, but they never, ever gave up, no matter what."

With those words, I realized that Mike was looking right at my father and me. I was speechless as he walked over to us with a big smile on his face. I took the bottle from his hand and, together with my father, unscrewed the cap and poured the contents into the Atlantic Ocean. The other riders clapped and cheered in honor of Team Wagner. As the applause went on, I looked at my father, and then at my family, and finally at my ABB teammates. I doubt there will be many moments in my life that will mean as much to me. I gathered my composure and thanked Mike for the honor of the water bottle and of riding with him. Jan popped open a bottle of champagne, and before I knew it a glass of bubbly was in my hand.

The next thirty minutes were a blur as families were introduced, riders hugged each other, more photographs were taken, and bicycles were finally wheeled off the sand. In keeping with my usual rear guard status, I was one of the last riders to leave the beach. With Shiva under my hand, I turned and looked back at the Atlantic Ocean. *From sea to shining sea.* I thought. *I did it.*

The Banquet

AFTER WE LEFT THE SHORELINE, MANY OF US STOPPED AT A BEACHFRONT bar to toss back a cold one. Between the champagne, the beer, and the long, hot shower I took once we got to our hotel, I was as relaxed as I'd been in a long time. The ABB team had reserved a large hall at the hotel for our farewell banquet. A few days earlier, Mike told us he was going to ask each of us to say a few words to the group about the ride. As the Wolf Pack made its way across the vineyards of New York, the Green Mountains of Vermont, and the rain-soaked streets of New Hampshire and Massachusetts, I thought about what I could possibly say to the other riders to let them know what this journey, as well as each of them, meant to me.

The banquet hall was beautiful with a huge cake in the corner that read, "Congratulations ABB Fast Track!" We all took seats at big round tables—tired, happy men with sunburns and raccoon eyes together with the families and the friends who loved them. Photographs of the ride were projected onto a screen at the front of the room, and riders smiled and pointed as they spotted themselves riding across the miles.

Mike opened the festivities with congratulations for all and told several stories about the trip. Hearing him speak, I realized how much I would miss his deep voice and his southern accent—and him. Then he told the audience that the riders would speak. I sat back and listened as each man addressed the room.

Big Tom hilariously demonstrated how a man with "lower region" soreness walks after a few days in the saddle. During our lunch in Kansas, he reminded me that you never know the story behind each person. Max spoke in the Australian accent I'd grown to love so much, focusing on each of us as he warmly thanked everyone for his or her support. I will always remember the time he told me he considered himself selfish because he wanted the most from every day. Greg pulled out a small cutout of a kitchen sink and announced to everyone that we'd carried "everything and the kitchen sink" across the United States. And when he started yodeling a song he called "Oh Lord My Aching Legs!" I thought I would burst from laughing. George complimented our country, saying how nice it was to trade the bustling traffic of London for the vast open spaces of the Midwest. Phil thanked everyone for the contributions to the Wounded Warrior Project. (During the ride he had planted the seed in my mind to do my part to honor our brave veterans.) When Tim addressed the audience wearing his Wolf Pack T-shirt, I don't know whose grin was bigger, my mother's or mine. Several other riders gave more reserved speeches, but all were sincere and heartfelt.

Mike looked my way and I knew it was my turn. "And now," he said, "meet the youngest rider in the group and one of the most impressive young men I have ever met. Eric Wagner."

I waited for the icy grip of fear I had felt the first time I met this group, but it never came. Mike placed the cordless microphone in my steady hand, and I stood and scanned the audience. There was fair-skinned Mark, who during April and May had singlehandedly kept the sunscreen business profitable; Richard, who'd taken time to show me how to properly climb hills; Little Tom, who'd ridden taller and stronger than almost anyone on the trip but still cared enough to help my father and me adjust our seats properly; Jan, our unofficial team doctor, who always made time to tend to the well-being of each rider, including my father and me.

I saw Big Dan, who shared his cookie with me on top of a mountain. I turned towards Floris, who had touched me with his incredible story of perseverance and had promised to send me one of his most prized jerseys, assuring me it would give me "magic legs." I remembered his powerful words during the T-shirt swap: "It's amazing what you can do when you stop listening to what others say is impossible." And I saw Jim J., who introduced me to butt paste and gave me a new way to appreciate the term *hero*; Philippe, who came to my rescue with the words "we are together"; Shane and Jody, strong riders whose unconventional training methods included cross-country skiing, rugby, and boxing; Norman, who despite having his bike destroyed in transit from Australia, remained positive and committed to the journey, purchasing a new bike right on the spot in Albuquerque.

Toward the back I saw Roger, whose partner had presented him with a beautiful hand-stitched tapestry of the complete ABB route across the country; David, who had ridden with the passion and the energy of men half his age. And finally, I saw my fellow Wolf Pack founder Joe, who despite having known me less than seventy-two hours never left my side when my father became sick and who by this time had become a close friend.

"Mom," I began casually, walking around the table, "would you mind taking a look at the clock over there and tell me what time it is?" My mother gave me a confused look as she followed my gesturing hand toward a mounted wall clock. I bent down so she could answer into the microphone. "It's almost nine o'clock," she said, her tone matching her uncertain expression.

"That's right. Nine o'clock," I repeated and turned back to the crowd. "In case you all didn't know, this is around the time my father, Joe, and I would be pulling into the motel parking lot. Because that's just how the Wolf Pack does it!" The banquet hall rang with laughter and howls. I walked away from the table toward the front of the room. With each step I felt like the Eric Wagner I used to know.

"I'd like to thank everyone in this room for helping me get through the past thirty-three days," I said. "I thank Mike for his humor and his passion for cycling and for getting us from the West

Coast to the East Coast safely. Barbara for feeding us every day with a smile on her face. Rest assured, I'll never eat again unless I've washed my hands. Karen for tirelessly guiding our cycling family to the Atlantic Ocean. And Jim for sharing stories with me and for keeping our bikes running in top shape. To my father, I will remember this trip with you for the rest of my life. There are no words to describe your dedication to me and to your family. And to my mom and brother, I am so happy you are here to share this moment. Your love and support mean the world to me, and I am a lucky young man to be a Wagner.

"You know," I went on, "my father always told me that if you want to succeed in life, you have to surround yourself with the kind of people who are willing to go that extra mile with you no matter what. Each of you did just that for me, metaphorically and physically, and I will never be able to thank you enough. I started out this ride with one amazing dad, and somehow I ended with a whole bunch more." I spoke for a few more minutes about some of my favorite memories from the trip, but when I heard my voice start to shake with emotion, I knew it was time to wrap it up. The clapping and the cheering went on even as I sat in my chair.

When the applause finally died down, Mike told the crowd, "Now you see what I mean about impressive, right? And here's the other half of Team Wagner—father Ralph." My father took the microphone, and his first words were "Well, you can tell that my son used to be in Drama Club, because that is one tough speech to follow. But I'll give it a try. I want to first thank the America by Bicycle team for the tremendous support every day of our epic ride across our great country. Second, I'd like to thank each of the riders with whom we shared the road these past thirty-three days for your camaraderie, your encouragement, and the many lessons you taught both my son and me.

"As a young man Eric's age, I chose to attend a military college and to pursue the life of an army officer. I came to understand the basic principles of success after college during ranger school in the summer of 1981. It was there I learned the meaning of leadership, teamwork, selflessness, honor, integrity, mission first, and your comrades always. These were lessons my father had tried to instill in me, and like most young men, I rarely wanted to listen. It wasn't until I experienced the fields of Georgia and the swamps of Florida that I found my own meaning of life.

"Eric was always a good athlete, a good student, and is an exceptional young man. But like many young people, he hit some bumps along the way—actually he hit some pretty big bumps. Eric learned many hard lessons his last two years in college, and when the time came for him to graduate he had his degree in hand, but I realized that he was still wrestling with many questions—namely, what happened to me in college? Who I am? I started to think how I could help Eric rebuild the confidence I knew was still in him. And then an idea came to me. Riding across the United States on my bicycle had always been a big dream of mine, so last August I asked Eric if he would like to join me, and as I had hoped, he jumped at the chance.

"The rest, as they say, is history. It was clear from the first day that Eric and I were the least experienced riders in the group. The advice you shared with us was invaluable, and how you all took Eric under your wings far surpassed my expectations. He has learned to overcome the fear of failure and realizes the importance of surrounding himself with people he can turn to. Because of all of you, I have seen Eric completely transformed. My son is back.

"It's been an honor riding with each of you in this room. I end with the ranger motto that means 'Of one's own will'—Sua Sponte!" The applause was deafening.

Good-Bye

I OPENED MY EYES AND GLANCED AT MY WATCH. IT WAS OBVIOUS I WAS still on ABB time because outside my window, the sky was completely black without a hint of approaching dawn. The rest of the world appeared to be fast asleep as my brother snored softly in the bed next to mine. I tried to grab a few more hours of sleep, but within five minutes I threw back the covers. I looked at my mesh shorts hanging on the back of a chair and at my running shoes under the bed. I hadn't done much running in the past year, and after so many miles on Shiva, I had no way of knowing how my tired legs would handle the stress. I just knew that the longer I stayed in bed, the more restless I would feel, so I quietly got dressed, put my iPod in my pocket, and slipped out the door.

The hotel was eerily silent as I stepped into an empty elevator and rode it down to the lobby. The front doors parted noiselessly, and as I stepped around fresh puddles, I realized it must have rained throughout the night. I put on my headphones, clicked on my music, and slowly began jogging. I didn't have a particular distance in mind or a route planned. All I knew was I had to keep moving forward. As I ran, my mind raced with one thought: *It's over. It's over. It's over.*

The world was quiet as I ran down street after street. My joints creaked in protest; my calves felt tight as snare drums. Sweat dripped down my face and soaked my shirt as the town of Amesbury slowly came to life with the light of the rising sun. I passed fast-food places, mom-and-pop stores, hotels, and houses. My body relished the old connection of my feet to the earth without tires in between, and the miles passed quickly, leading me back to where I had started. My legs were shaky as I slowed to a walk outside of the hotel to take a few cool-down laps. My heart rate and my breathing began returning to normal, and as I rounded the corner to the back of the building, I stopped in my tracks. Just like the night I arrived in California, parked in the very back of the lot, was the blue ABB luggage trailer.

I clicked off my music and walked over to the trailer. The morning dew glistened on its metallic surface, and droplets slid down the ABB logo. I stared at it for a few minutes and then slowly lifted my hand and pressed my palm against its cool metal.

How could I have known what was in store for me the first time I saw it? I remembered how frantic I was to find the answers to a life that had seemingly gone way off track. I'd ridden more than 3,400 miles through fourteen states only to discover that what I'd been so desperately seeking couldn't be found in the vast expanse of mountains, flatlands, rivers, highways, and backcountry roads. The answers didn't lie beneath the waves of the Pacific or the Atlantic oceans, either.

I realized that what I'd been seeking all along was a clear, definitive, and easy road map to life. The trip had shown me with great clarity that such road maps do not exist. The reality is that sometimes life is a tangled mess. There will be tough hills to climb, detours that take you off course, and winds threatening to knock you over. And sometimes life is joy beyond words. There will be majestic views if you take the time to see them, warm cookies to share, and family and friends who race to your side when you're in trouble. The most important thing I learned on my *Leaving It on the Road* journey was that my *it* was fear—fear of failure, fear of judgment, fear of my own face in the mirror, and fear of an empty epitaph after living a life that didn't resemble me. Somewhere in my college years, fear began running my life, and the moment I'd let it take the wheel, my identity had begun to unravel. I had left bits and pieces of my fear on every quiet country road, busy highway, college bike path, and city street until it was just about gone. And now, standing next to the ABB trailer, I would leave the last bit of it in that hotel parking lot.

Did I have all the answers to my life? No. Not even close. But at long last, I had the courage to start looking for them—without fear. And that was enough for now. I patted the trailer's metal flanks and silently mouthed the word *good-bye*. I dropped my hand down, stepped back, and turned toward the hotel. It was time to go home.

George in small-town America.

No matter how many milkshakes he drank, my father
seemed to be disappearing before my eyes.

My good friend, Noelle.

This sign should say Welcome to Pennsylvania
AGAIN Ralph, Eric, and Joe.

As promised, Floris sent me his magic jersey after the trip.

Finally a familiar city.

My favorite photograph of the entire ride.

Grass-fed burgers before a five-mile climb... not so smart.

Left to right: Me, my father, Barry, George, and Richard.

Our last group photograph before reaching our destination.

The very last mile.

Barry's bear heading towards the Atlantic Ocean.

Hello Atlantic Ocean.

The honor of the water bottle.

From sea to shining sea!

A beautiful gift to Roger during the banquet.

Epilogue

THIS IS THE PART WHERE I TALK TO YOU, MY READERS, ABOUT WHAT I'VE learned since the day I left that hotel parking lot. You might be expecting me to offer some additional deep-seated wisdom that I gained during those five long weeks sharing the road with my father and the rest of the ABB team—how I've applied that knowledge to grow into a better version of myself than when we headed out from the Pacific beach on the morning of April 21, 2013. But if there's one thing I've learned about life, it's that it never plays out exactly the way you'd expect.

Real life doesn't wrap up neatly at the conclusion of a journey with credits rolling and music playing as you ride off triumphantly into the sunset. This isn't Hollywood, and we aren't at the theater, so if you're looking for some philosophical epiphany, you won't find it here. What you will find, however, is that the answer to life, as I've come to know it, is far simpler than you could ever have imagined. There is no complex riddle to be solved nor some mysterious insight that will instantly lead you down the road to happiness. Trust me—I looked for it the whole time I was riding those 3,400 miles across the United States.

Instead, in the months after the ride ended, I learned that the answers to those questions I had been asking had existed within me the whole time. Now, I know you're probably thinking that sounds a little clichéd, perhaps something Dorothy realized before clicking her red shoes and catching the next balloon out of Oz. Yet sometimes the simplest truths are the ones with the most impact.

Back in my junior year of college, I came to believe that I was incapable of becoming more than the unrecognizable version of myself sitting alone in my dark room. In the deepest part of my heart, I believed that the young man I had once been was lost forever. All of the demons that had taken up residence in my mind refused to allow me to see past anything other than what they wanted me to see. My biggest demon, fear, had blinded me to the answers I desperately sought. It did everything in its power to keep me alone in that room. But by making the difficult choice to ask for help, and then just as important accepting that help from family and friends, I gained the courage to begin taking control of my life again. But as you read in my story, this certainly didn't happen all at once. Just as with the bike ride, I sometimes operated minute by minute, repeating the same thing I said making my way up the tallest mountains: "Just get to that point. Okay, now just get to that point."

Since the end of the ride, I've run a marathon, fallen in love with a wonderful girl whom I got to know at a party my mom threw for my father and me after the trip (Shiva will definitely be at the wedding!), and have challenged myself on all fronts of life. I'm now a spin instructor and certified personal fitness trainer committed to helping others find their best health, because I passionately believe physical, emotional, and mental health are intricately connected. I continue to be relentlessly honest with myself, unafraid to ask the same questions I asked myself in Dalhart, Texas, with unflinching resolution.

Who am I? What kind of person do I want to be? How can I help others who might be struggling?

New answers continue to present themselves every day. My name is Eric Wagner. I'm not perfect, and that's okay. I care deeply and feel passionately about what I do with my life and how it affects those around me. Just like everyone else, I am sometimes scared and feel uncertain about my future. But now I am willing to be honest and to ask for help when those fears, uncertainties, and doubts begin to feel overwhelming. I seek out people in my life I trust for guidance and for reassurance. I learn something new every day, and I figure out how to make the next day better.

Riding a bicycle across the United States can't happen in a single day, and neither can a transformation of your life. You need time, patience, and the support of others to make a lasting difference in the way you view the world and what is possible. And believe me—it doesn't take an epic adventure to change your life. It takes the decision to change it.

My wish for you, my readers, is that you will walk away from reading *Leaving It on the Road* and be willing to ask yourself, what is my *it*? What is it that might be holding me back from the dreams I once held so dear? If this book serves as a first step toward your own journey of self-discovery as you begin to leave whatever your *it* is far behind you, then I will have done what I set out to do.

Thank you so much for coming along with me on my journey. I hope I hear from you one day.

About the Author

Leaving It on the Road is Eric Wagner's debut memoir. Passionate about fitness and writing, Eric graduated from James Madison University with a degree in journalism and creative writing. He is a blogger, a spin instructor, and a certified personal fitness trainer dedicated to unlocking each client's physical and mental potential. You can visit him at www.LeavingItontheRoad.com.

One last thing …

If you'd like more information on my friends and their websites, here's a list:

Floris—http://www.overveld.net

Barry—http://www.saveonelife.net/wheels-for-the-world-fundraiser-biking-2015.php

Phil—http://philsepicadventures.blogspot.com

America by Bicycle—http://americabybicycle.com

Brian Drury—http://overcominggraduation.com

Marty's Reliable Cycle—http://martysreliable.com/articles/contact-us-pg32.htm

Zack Ayers—http://zackayers.com

Treasures of a Nurse's Heart: My Mother's Memoirs of Love and Wisdom for Everyday Life—http://www.barnesandnoble.com/w/treasures-of-a-nurses-heart-lisa-smith-wagner/1120571756?ean=9780595377152

Printed in the United States
By Bookmasters